GOING PAST THE

Darkness

AND INTO THE

Light

EVELYN SCULL

ISBN 978-1-0980-8169-0 (paperback)
ISBN 978-1-0980-8170-6 (digital)

Christian Faith Publishing, Inc.
832 Park Avenue
Meadville, PA 16335
www.christianfaithpublishing.com

Printed in the United States of America

CONTENTS

INTRODUCTION

What is faith? Is there anyone who really understands faith? It is a believing without proof, trust, confidence, reliance, doing one's duty, and keeping one's promises. Actually believing in someone is the same thing as having faith. What do we say then about someone who is faithless—they are unworthy of trust, failing in one's duty, breaking one's promises.

In everyone's life, at one time or another, they hold on to faith. They either put their faith in someone else or they put their faith in Father (God). We, as humans, would like to believe that we're independent of others, but in reality, we're not. Every time a person goes to a bank and puts their money in a savings or a checking account, they are putting their faith in the bank to watch over their money so when they need it, it will be there. When you send a child off to school to learn, you're trusting the teacher to teach your child to the best of their ability.

Who believes in faith? Everyone! Most people won't admit that they have faith, but sooner or later we all do. The sad part is that some people have faith for the wrong reasons. There are those that only have faith in themselves. They believe that the only person they can trust is themselves, but it's not always true. Most people don't realize that they abuse their souls more than they abuse their bodies.

If you believe you have a soul, then you must also believe in Father (God), and that's where faith begins. Not everyone believes in Father; at least they don't think they do, but in a way by having faith that is exactly what they are doing. This book is based on that faith. Just so the reader understands, I do not call God God. To me, he turned out to be much more than that—I call him Father. Soon, when both books are finished, you will understand why.

This is a book about two women: one about a woman who struggles through her life but never lost her faith and one about another woman who lost her faith only to find it again through someone else whom she came to love. These stories should touch your heart and your mind.

The book is named *Going Past the Darkness and into the Light* because of what one of the women discovers. The stories, however, have each their own name not only to separate them but to let you know where one ends and where the other begins. If you keep your mind open, you will be able to see the connection between the two women.

At the beginning of each story, I tell you a little bit about them and let you keep a couple of questions in your mind to think about while you're reading them. Let's see what answers you come up with at the end. Maybe by the time you get to the end, those questions will have answers. I hope you enjoy the book.

The Miracle

In 1967, the medical technology wasn't as advanced as it is now, thirty years later. We have more machines and equipment than we ever thought possible back then. The more years that pass us by, the more technology humans will create, which will give us more ways to help save human lives from disease and illness.

You have to think about this woman and the chances she would have survived back then. Here are the two questions you must ask yourself:

> Is it the medical technology that saved her life?
> Or
> Is it her faith that saved her?

CHAPTER 1

The Tragedy of Becoming Sick

It's a beautiful spring day. The temperature is just right, and there is a nice little breeze. You find yourself standing on a sidewalk of a street that has four corners. The street is somewhat busy. You see children crossing the corner coming home from school. On one of the corners is a fire station. Across the street from that is a white house. On the corner, you seem to be standing on is a big gray house.

While you're looking at the gray house, here is what you notice. In front, there is a porch with bushes around it. On one side of the house, there is a row of flower bushes. On the other side of the house, there is a concrete driveway. Then beside the driveway, there is an enormous tree where part of it hangs over the street. You look up at the tree and you see that the house is two stories, almost looks to be as tall as the tree is.

Then as you are standing there, you hear somebody singing. You decide to see where it's coming from so you walk up the concrete driveway. At the beginning of the driveway, there is a two-car garage that is white. You then see the back of the house. There is a stairway on the outside that leads to a door on the second story. Then you see a yard with children playing in it.

One is a little boy who is four years old. We will call him Jack. Jack has black hair and brown eyes. He is a very scrawny looking boy. The other child in the yard is his sister Amanda; she's about two years old. She has dark brown hair and blue eyes. She still has some of her baby fat. You can still hear the singing so you're wondering who it is. You realize the singing is coming from inside the house.

So you decide to open the door on the first floor and take a peek inside. It seems to be a very old house. The doorways are round instead of square. You walk through the back door and there are two sets of stairs; a long set that looks to lead to the basement and another one that is four or five steps that lead to an inside door of the house. You open the door at the top of those steps. On the left, there is another door that is closed. On the right, there is a little hallway that goes to a bathroom. In front of you, there is a kitchen.

Now you see the person who is singing. A very pretty woman, who looks to be about thirty-five years old, she has coal black hair that is shiny and brown eyes. Her name is Mary. Inside the house with her is a much older man, about fifty-nine years old. You're thinking that is probably her father. He has gray hair, is very stocky, and you can tell he is German. His name is Kyle.

You finally realize that Kyle isn't Mary's father, but her husband, and you're thinking, *What an odd couple*. You can also tell they are very much in love with each other. Mary is a very sweet woman. When people would come to the door asking for donations she would be very happy to give one. She is considered to be a housewife, but before she met Kyle she was going to church college in California where they met each other.

Mary stays home every day and does the cooking, cleaning, and taking care of the children. Kyle, though, owned his own business and provided for her and the children. He was raised during the time where a man provided for this family. He owns houses and real estate all over the city they lived in, and not only there, but in other states too. During the week, they take care of what they are both supposed to take care of and on Sundays, they go to church.

Not everybody approves of them being together because of the difference in their ages. They think he is too old for her and she has no business marrying an older man. They think she is too young for him and he has no business marrying a younger woman. His family, brothers, sisters, and his three older children from his first marriage refuse to talk to him very often because of her. Her family, father, mother, brother, sister, and oldest son from her first marriage refuse to talk to her because of him.

Both of them had previously been married and both of their spouses had died. Both his and her families held resentments. So it seems that Kyle and Mary are all alone, except for their two children. Jack was from the first marriage but little Amanda is the only child they had together. Since not everybody accepted them, they didn't go to church in the town they lived in, instead, they would drive to a town called Monticello.

There was a church there that accepted them both. The preacher would say it does not matter what age you are or how different you are, that God loves everyone just the way they are. If two people loved each other enough then that is all that matters. Now the church is old but it is a very nice church. On the inside of the church, there are rows of benches made of old wood, which are very shiny and very pretty.

There is an aisle that separates them both, and at the end of the aisle is a pillar. Behind the pillar, there is a place where the choir stood. Mary, who loves to sing, is a member of the choir. There is nothing that could keep them from going to church on Sundays. The two of them had a lot of faith. They believed that God brought them together for a purpose and that they would be together forever till they died.

Later on, it is discovered what that purpose ended up being. One thing is for sure, if we learn anything at all, it is that you should never question why things happen the way they do because truly Father does have a reason for everything that does take place.

We are back in the kitchen now with Mary. She's standing there getting dinner ready and Kyle walks in.

Kyle says, "Hi, honey! When is dinner going to be ready?"

As she's turning the fire down on the stove, she says, "It will be done in about five minutes."

Kyle says, "Great! I'm hungry. I will go outside and tell the children to come in and wash their hands for dinner."

As a family, they always sit down to eat dinner together. At night time, Mary would always sing Amanda to sleep. Then she would go in and tuck Jack in bed.

The next day, Kyle goes off to work just like he did every day. It always seems like it was the same routine day after day. Mary would get up and make breakfast for her family. She would send her husband off to work and take care of the children. Mary knew it was Jack's birthday and she wanted to get him something special. Mary gets a babysitter to watch the children, so she could go shopping.

During Jack's birthday party, Kyle noticed there was something wrong with Mary. Her hand kept shaking when she was trying to cut the cake.

After the party is over, Kyle says to Mary, "Are you feeling okay? I noticed your hand was shaking earlier."

Mary says to him, "I have a really bad headache and I am having a real hard time controlling my hands today."

Kyle answers and says, "I think you should go and see the doctor tomorrow."

So the next day Mary goes to see a doctor. She is sitting in the waiting room when her head starts to hurt again. She gets called in to the patient room by the nurse.

The nurse says to her, "How are you today?"

Mary replies and says, "I would be fine if I could get rid of this headache."

So the nurse does what most nurses do. Takes her temperature, blood pressure, and then leaves the room. The nurse didn't want to say anything to Mary, but her blood pressure seemed kind of high. She thought she would let the doctor do that. Mary is sitting there looking at a magazine when the doctor comes in.

The doctor says, "Hello, Mary. What seems to be the problem?"

Mary smiles and answers him, "I have really bad headaches lately and sometimes I can't control my hand from shaking, plus I drop things."

Then the doctor says, "We better take a look at you then."

When the doctor comes back in, he says, "Mary, I think I found your problem. You seem to have high blood pressure. I'm going to put you on some medicine that you are to take every day. This should stop you from having headaches."

The doctor didn't say anything about her having problems holding on to things. Mary just assumed that it was because of the high blood pressure. When she was done, she drives home to start making dinner. Just like she always did every day.

A couple of days later, she gets another really bad headache. She just assumes since she was late in taking her medicine that is probably what caused it. After nine months passed, she is still getting her headaches but didn't want to tell anyone. Worse is that she is dropping things, and passing out, and not telling anyone.

Then one day, on March 19, 1967, they are all sitting and watching television.

Kyle says to her, "Would you please get me a cup of coffee?"

So she walks into the kitchen and starts pouring it when all of a sudden Kyle and the children heard a loud crash. So they all three came running into the kitchen.

"Are you okay, Mary?" Kyle asks.

Mary answers him and says, "Sorry, I dropped the coffee pot, broke it, and cut my hand."

So Kyle tells Jack, "Go and get the first aid kit."

Jack says, "Okay, Daddy. I'll get it."

While Kyle is bandaging up Mary's hand, the children walk back into the family room. Amanda, being only three years old, looks at Jack and says, "Is Mommy, okay?"

Jack simply says, "She just cut her hand. I think she will be okay." Jack, however, was concerned too.

Kyle notices she is acting really moody lately. Snapping at people and not really acting like she normally does. He decides it is best not to say anything for now. Over the next three months, she keeps getting worse. She is dropping things, yelling, and screaming like she is out of her mind.

Then one day, on June 22, 1967, just like normal, Kyle goes to work. He doesn't realize what he is going to find when he came home that day.

When Jack gets home from a summer camp, he goes to his mom and says, "Can I spend the night at Mike's house?"

"Sure, Jack, if that's what you want to do," Mary answers him with a smile.

So Mike's parents come and pick up Jack. Amanda was the only one home now with her mother. They had fun though; they played games and made cupcakes. Kyle had a long day at work and is very tired so all he could think about is getting home, eating, and going to bed. When he walks in through the back door around 8:00 p.m., he heard Amanda crying. So he walks up the stairway to the other door, opens it, and before his eyes, he sees Mary lying on the floor. Amanda is crying over her.

Amanda is saying, "Please, Mommy, get up."

She looks up at her father and says, "Mommy won't wake up, Daddy."

"Oh my god, Mary! Amanda, what happened?" Kyle is stunned about what he saw. He reaches out for Mary to make sure she is still breathing. He runs out of the house to the fire station across the street. He lets the firemen know that his wife isn't moving. So they rush out the door with their equipment following Kyle.

When they get into the house, one of them calls for an ambulance, two of them start checking Mary, and the fourth one goes over to Amanda.

"Can you tell me how long your mother's been lying there?"

Amanda who is still unsure about what is going on says, "For a little while."

The ambulance finally gets there and takes Mary to the hospital.

The next day in the hospital, she's doing better. The doctor comes into the room.

"Hi, Mary, I am Dr. Steiner. How are you feeling this morning?"

She looks at him with this pale look and says, "Can you tell me what happened to me? The last thing I remember is I was playing in the house with Amanda."

He looks at her, smiles, and says, "Well let's keep you for a couple of days and run some tests to see what we can find out."

So Mary agrees to stay for a few days. The doctors run test after test but could not find anything abnormal. Finally, they decide to let her go home. They change her medication, hoping that would take care of the problem. Unfortunately, that is only the beginning of things to come.

CHAPTER 2

The Choice

It's Christmas Day 1969. By now, Amanda is four and a half years old. Jack had just turned seven years old back in June. Mary is thirty-seven and Kyle is sixty-one. They sit around the Christmas tree and open their presents. The living room has a fireplace that was very cozy. They also eat fudge that Mary makes every year. It seems to be the perfect Christmas. The whole day is very special. Mary still sometimes had problems and is in and out of the hospital on various occasions.

Mary seems to be doing well. She didn't have any headaches, at least lately, and she hadn't dropped anything all day. That night, after everybody goes to sleep, Mary sits by the fireplace and says a little prayer. "Lord, I don't know why this is happening to me and I know it is not for me to question what your plan is for me, but whatever is wrong with me, there has to be a reason for it."

Christmas Day came and went. It's New Year's Eve 1969. Mary and Kyle sit by the fireplace holding each other, talking, laughing, and remembering when they first met. Mary decides she would get up and check on the children to make sure they were sound asleep in their beds. All of a sudden, she starts feeling funny. Then she passes out and hits the floor.

Kyle thinks he heard something, so he calls out Mary's name, "Mary," but there seems to be no answer. He gets up to go see what the noise was that he heard and he finds Mary lying on the floor. He picks up the phone and he calls for help. The firemen across the street were the first ones to respond. Once Mary is on her way to the hospital, Kyle takes the children to someone who could watch them. He had no way of knowing how long he would be there.

When he gets back home, he decides that it is time to let the rest of the family know what is going on. The doctors start running more tests again to see if they could figure out what is wrong. So far, they didn't have any luck. Way back then, they did not have the best testing like they do now.

When Kyle finally gets a hold of her brother in Washington DC, he tells him that the doctors here could not seem to figure out the problem even after so many tests. Her brother is very worried about Mary and wonders if she would be okay. He knew a brain specialist that lived in the DC area and asked him if he would look at his sister's case. So Kyle and Mary's brother paid to fly him to where Kyle was living.

Kyle is so upset over what is going on with Mary that he keeps praying to God that Mary would be okay. He loves her very much and didn't want her to be sick. He could not understand why this is happening to them. Kyle always tried to be faithful to God and he thinks maybe this was a test of his faith.

The brain specialists that Mary's brother had gotten flies to Illinois, where Kyle lived; his name was Dr. Fairchild. Dr. Fairchild was the best in his field and if anybody could find the problem, he could.

When he arrives in Illinois, he goes straight to the hospital. He brings equipment that the other doctors had never seen before, with analyzing machines with gadgets and other very strange things.

He does blood tests and what he calls a brain scan. When he did all the tests he wanted to do, he calls her brother and Kyle. He tells them he knows what's wrong with Mary. Dr. Fairchild didn't think it was a good idea to tell them what was wrong with her over the phone. He thinks it would be best to tell them in person.

He tells Kyle if there was anybody else he felt should be there then he should call them now. So Kyle gets on the phone and calls

Mary's stepmother and father. He tells them if they wanted to know what is wrong with their daughter that the doctor is going to meet with them tomorrow at eleven o'clock in the morning. They lived in Washington State, which is pretty far away, but they tell Kyle they would catch the first flight out.

After Kyle gets off the phone with her parents, he calls Mary's sister in Michigan and tells her the same thing. She also says that she will be there as soon as she could. The last person he was to get a hold of is the most difficult to talk to, which is her oldest son, Jeremy. You see, he is living with Mary's dead husband's sister, and they didn't like Kyle at all, worse than anybody else in either one of the families. No matter what their personal opinion was about her marrying Kyle, they still think they should be there.

All the family gathers together at the hospital. The brain specialist comes into the room where they all were sitting and waiting.

He walks in and says, "Good morning, my name is Dr. Fairchild. I'm glad you could all make it. I don't know how to tell you this, so I'll just come out and say it. Mary has a tumor right above her main artery to her brain, which is causing the circulation to be cut off to her brain."

He continues to say, "We can operate and remove it, but there is a danger in doing so. She could die from having the surgery done. If she doesn't have the surgery, though, she will surely die in the next few months. So you, as her family, are the only ones that can sign the papers. You need to make a decision."

Her brother speaks up and says, "Is there any other way?"

"No, I'm sorry. You must make sure that you let me know your answer as soon as possible. Every day we wait, the greater the chance there is she won't pull through."

So they all go in to see Mary, and then they all leave and meet at Kyle and Mary's house. They all decide to discuss what they think they should do; now there were a whole bunch of arguments about it.

Mary's stepmother says, "Let us give her that two months or so to live, at least it's better than having the surgery and dying now."

Then Kyle spoke up and said, "What if the surgery saves her life and it gives her a chance to live?"

Then Mary's sister says, "What if it doesn't and she dies having it done?"

Anyway, they go back and forth yelling at each other and arguing, and the children could hear them and it is really upsetting to little Amanda. Amanda is very smart for her age. All of a sudden Amanda decides to walk into the room where they were and says, "Stop it! Why don't you ask Mommy what she wants?" You could see the tears rolling down her cheek.

I don't think the adults realized till that moment that it really isn't their decision. It is Mary's decision, even though she isn't capable of signing the papers herself. Mary could talk, she just isn't able to move very well. The tumor is paralyzing her.

So Kyle leaves the house to go see her. He goes into the intensive care unit where she is at. He sees that Mary is sleeping so he waits until she is awake. She is very weak, pale-looking, and she could not really do anything on her own, like sit up or feed herself.

When she wakes up, she sees Kyle and says, "Hi! I thought everybody left."

"They did, but I came back to talk to you alone," Kyle explains to her.

Mary says, "What's wrong? I can see something is bothering you. Did the doctors tell you what they found out because they have not told me anything yet?"

Kyle says to her, "Yes. The doctors discovered you have a tumor and you don't have much time. Everybody at the house has been arguing whether or not you should have the surgery. Then your daughter walked into the room and yelled at all of us. She said it was your decision. We all realized she was right. We didn't even stop to think about how you might feel about it."

Mary knew what Kyle is trying to say, so she answers him and says, "That's okay, I understand how everybody feels. They are just scared and so am I."

Kyle looks at her, a little scared to ask this question, "Mary, what is it that you want? The doctor says you could die during surgery."

Mary responds knowing she has faith in God. "I think I will leave my life in the hands of God and have the surgery done."

"Are you sure that is what you want?" Kyle says to her with a tear running down his face.

"Yes, if I die, then I know it was God's will," she says with a smile.

Kyle says goodnight to Mary and tells her he will see her in the morning. When he gets back to the house, he tells the family what her decision is. They are not too happy about it but they have to stand by what she wants.

The next day, the family get together at the hospital in the waiting room. They are all sitting there wondering if Mary will pull through the surgery. Just about five hours later, the doctor walks into the waiting room and says, "I'm sorry, we lost her."

Kyle is so upset he goes straight to the chapel in the hospital, falls to his knees and says, "Why, Lord, why?" Then the tears just flowed from his eyes.

Then he says, "Take my life instead, Lord, not hers, please don't take her from me. I will give up everything I own so she may live."

In the waiting room with the rest of the family, they all could not believe how this could happen. They are saying she should not have had the surgery. Dr. Fairchild, feeling really bad, says, "I'm sorry. I did everything I could."

Dr. Fairchild walks out of the waiting room and goes back into the operating room to take one last look at Mary. He thinks about what he could have done differently to save her when all of a sudden her heart monitor beeped. At first, he thinks he is seeing things but then he also thinks that is impossible because she had been dead for over ten minutes by now. Then he sees it beep again. He yells for the nurse and she comes in.

The nurse says, "What is it you need, Doctor?"

"Help me," the doctor states to the nurse.

So they start an oxygen machine back up on her and her heart beat becomes stronger.

The doctor says, "I don't believe in miracles but this truly has got to be one. She is alive please go tell the family."

The doctor thinks how long Mary would be able to live because the oxygen had been cut off from her brain for ten minutes or more. Yes, her heart was beating again but she was in a coma.

In the chapel where Kyle was sitting on his knees crying, her brother walks in saying, "Mary's alive! It's a miracle she came back." Kyle gets up from being on his knees and goes straight to her.

The doctor decides he better talk with the family and explain to them about Mary, and what condition she is in. So he tells the nurse to go tell the family that he would like to speak to all of them.

A few minutes, later the doctor comes into the waiting room.

He says, "Hi! I don't know how but her heart started beating again. The problem is that she is in a coma. I don't know for how long or if she will ever wake up again. She isn't breathing normally on her own. We have an oxygen machine helping her breathe. She lost a lot of oxygen to her brain for at least ten minutes or more, so we can't be certain as to what effect this will have on her. She may wake up again, but there is always the possibility that she may never wake up at all."

Kyle speaks up and says, "How long before we know?"

Dr. Fairchild says, "I'm not really sure. It could be a week, a month, but one thing is for sure, if she doesn't come out of her coma within the next two months, the chances are she never will. If she doesn't come out of her coma, there would be no reason to keep her alive on oxygen since she can't breathe or function on her own. Another consideration is that it could be possible that when she wakes up, she might have brain damage. Loss of speech and the ability to do things without assistance is a probability."

So the whole family just says there is nothing we can do but wait and pray. So the doctor suggests to her family that they go home, wait, and he would let them know if there is any change in Mary's condition. So Mary's brother, and sister, and parents go back home to where they lived. They know there is nothing they could do for her. Kyle promises them that he would keep in touch and so he does.

CHAPTER 3

Close to Death

Kyle has a hard time explaining to the children about their mother. The children try really hard to understand. The two months passed and still there was no change in Mary's condition. At this time, the medical bills has reached a significant amount. It was over a quarter of a million dollars. Kyle has no medical insurance on Mary. So he sells some of his property to pay the hospital bills.

Kyle didn't care though because it was keeping Mary alive. Then one day the doctor calls from Washington DC and says they needed to talk. So Kyle says he would meet with him. Now Kyle has an idea as to what the doctor was going to say and he is upset even thinking about it.

The next day, Kyle goes to the hospital to see Mary just like he's done every day since she became ill. Dr. Fairchild flies to Illinois so he could to talk to Kyle. After Kyle was done visiting with Mary, he meets with Dr. Fairchild in the hospital.

"Hi, Kyle, how are you today?" Dr. Fairchild says with a smile.

Kyle says, "I'm okay, but there seems to be no change in Mary is there?"

"No. I'm sorry. I have been keeping in touch with the hospital there about her condition. I know you don't want to hear this, but Mary's still not breathing by herself without the machine. If she has not awakened up by now or started breathing on her own I don't think she ever will. So I think it's time you make a decision," the doctor explains.

Kyle hated to admit it, but the doctor is right. So they both came to the conclusion that they are going to unplug the breathing machine. So Kyle calls the family and tells them what they were about to do. It is Kyle's decision more than anyone else's. So Kyle then goes into Mary's room bends down beside her and clutches her hand as the doctor unplugs the machine.

Kyle's tears just flow from his eyes, and then he starts praying for her life. "Lord, please I don't want her to die on me."

The doctor is standing there with a stethoscope, waiting for her heart to stop beating. Then he sees her chest rise up and down. Kyle is still crying clutching Mary's hand and looking into her face.

Dr. Fairchild says, "Look, Kyle."

Then Kyle looks down at her chest. He sees it rise up and down too.

He says to Dr. Fairchild, "Does that mean what I think it means?"

"Yeah, she's breathing on her own," the doctor answers Kyle. You could see a tear come rolling down his cheek too. Then the doctor checks her real carefully and sees though that she's still in a coma.

Kyle says, "Is this a good sign?"

The doctor says, "For the moment, yes. As long as she continues to breathe on her own, then that's always a good sign. Now I know your medical expenses are getting really high. So I have a suggestion for you. It would be cheaper for you to take Mary to a nursing home or figure out a way to bring her home and get a nurse for her. Maybe someone who is retired could help you out."

The next day Kyle starts making inquiries about what he needed to do to have a nurse living in his home. So he sits down and makes a game plan on what he wanted to do first. The first thing he needed to do was to remodel his home. Kyle's house is two stories with an inside stairway leading upstairs and an outside stairway to the second floor for a fire escape. Inside the house, there are six bedrooms, two bathrooms, kitchen, living room, office, and a playroom. So he decides to change the upstairs of the house that had three of the bedrooms, bathroom, playroom, an office into an apartment instead.

Kyle takes the office out and makes it into a kitchen. Then he takes the playroom out and makes it into a living room, but he did keep the bedrooms just the way they were. So now he has a three-bedroom apartment for someone who might want to take the job to be Mary's nurse. The apartment looks really nice.

The next day Kyle puts up posters saying: "Needed retired nurse willing to take care of a comatose victim, includes a rent-free three bedroom apartment, free electricity, and water plus I am willing to pay a salary. For more information call 321-1234."

A few days later, he gets a phone call from a nurse who retired six months earlier. She has no husband and all her children are grown, except one grandchild who stays with her who was seventeen years old. So Kyle thinks she would be perfect for Mary. She would have somebody there that wouldn't be distracted all the time and would actually be able to keep a close eye on Mary.

So he meets with the nurse, shows her the apartment, and she takes the job. Her name is Sarah. Sarah will be able to watch Mary every day from 8:00 a.m. until about 5:00 p.m., seven days a week. Sarah thinks it is worth it because she didn't have to pay any bills at all.

Everything is now set for Mary to come home from the hospital. Everybody seems to be glad that she is finally coming home, especially the children. When she gets settled in, everything looks like it is going to work out fine. Sarah, the nurse, seemed to take real good care of her. She keeps an eye on her just like she promised to.

On May 10, 1972, three years after Mary's surgery, Sarah is taking care of Mary, like she always did every day. Now by this time Kyle is going on sixty-four, Mary is forty, Jack is nine years old, and little Amanda is seven. Kyle is at work and the children just get home from school about an hour ago. Sarah hears something coming from Mary's room. So she stops what she is doing to go and check on Mary.

When Sarah gets into Mary's room, she notices that the oxygen hose that Mary had in her nose had been removed. Mary has an oxygen tank next to the bed that keeps air going into her nose from it even though Mary could breathe on her own because she still is in a coma and they need to keep oxygen on her.

Sarah is standing there looking at her and goes to put it back in, then she gets the shock of her life. Mary opens her eyes and Sarah just about falls over. She couldn't believe it.

Mary says to her, "My daughter needs me." She gets right out of bed, walks outside where Amanda was laying in the driveway with her leg stuck in the spokes of her bike. Mary bends over, untangles Amanda's leg, and passes out in the driveway. During this time, Sarah is calling for an ambulance. She explains to them that she had a patient that just woke up out of a coma and needed assistance.

When Kyle gets home he couldn't believe it. He goes straight to the hospital the moment he is told she is awake. Dr. Fairchild receives a phone call from the hospital telling him about his patient. Every three months he had flown to Illinois and checked up on Mary and kept in contact with the nurse that Kyle had hired for her. Once he hears Mary is awake, he takes the first flight out to go to Illinois.

The first thing they did was run more tests; they wanted to see how much damage there was to her. What is interesting is the test showed that twenty percent of her brain tissue was dead, and so the doctor tells Kyle that she probably would never be the same again. What happened later is that the part of her brain that was not damaged takes over the parts of her brain that were. The tissue is healing. The doctors could not believe what they are witnessing. The doctors say they had never seen anything like it.

Mary still struggles with talking; she is slurring her words and is not able to do other daily things. It is a long road to recovery, which takes another four years. Every day she goes through therapy. They start with her speech first, working on the letters of the alphabet and having her try and put words together. Over time she learns to talk real good. Amanda goes into her mother's room and reads to her every day after school. Even though it was a miracle that day that she got out of bed and walked to her daughter who was crying outside, she still has mobility problems. Over time, they work on that too. Most people say it was her daughter's agonizing cries that woke her up.

One day during therapy, she says to Kyle, "I don't think I can do this."

Kyle replies and says to her, "I know you can, Mary. You have to try, please for me and if not for me for your children."

She keeps falling down but every time Kyle would try and pick her up and the nurse says to him, "You have to let her go, she won't succeed if you keep helping her."

So Mary keeps trying and the moment she is able to do things on her own, she starts crying. Everybody is so happy for her. She never gave up and has so much courage after everything she had been through.

A year later, she could do everything she could do before her tumor. She had one problem. They call it a mental defect even though her body was normal because her memory and ability to think is not always clear. She says things and does things that most people think is not normal behavior. A lot of the time she doesn't know what she is saying or a lot of the time people just don't understand her.

Sarah realizes she is not needed anymore, so she moves out of the apartment and goes to live someplace else by herself. Her only grandson that did live with her is married now and on his own. Sarah keeps in touch with Mary over the years until Sarah dies.

Mary has problems telling the difference between reality and non-reality sometimes. Amanda has just turned eleven years old when Sarah left. Amanda starts taking care of her mother instead. Kyle would get up before dawn and work till dusk. Amanda would cook, clean, and take care of her mother. She does everything she could to help her mother and to become an adult. Pretty much her childhood or what was supposed to be of it is taken from her. She even starts working a job, yes a job, but she has to lie about her age to get it. She would work Saturdays and Sundays, on the days her dad didn't work.

During the day, while Amanda is in school, Mary stays alone downstairs. Kyle rented the upstairs apartment to another family, who would check in on Mary from time to time, If Mary needs anything, she could just yell upstairs and Debbie, who is the tenant, would come down and help her. The children get home from school at around three in the afternoon every day. Kyle works really long hours; he sometimes didn't come home until eight or nine o'clock at night.

It is Amanda's responsibility to come home from school, do her homework, clean the house, and make dinner. As the days and years go by, Mary starts getting better and better.

In 1981, Amanda is sixteen; Jack is nineteen and isn't living at home anymore. Kyle is seventy-three and Mary is forty-nine years old. Mary is able to totally do everything on her own again. She could cook, clean, and she is much better mentally. She would slip once in a while and forget things but she seems to be doing well.

Amanda decides since her father is getting up there in years and her mother is able to take care of herself again that it is time for her to move out on her own. So Amanda finds a job and an apartment and pays for her last two years in high school. She understands the financial burden that her father has because of her mother's illness and she didn't want to burden him too.

The only thing he has left as far as all the property he had previously owned is two houses, one of which Amanda is buying from him. Amanda finally get married and has a family of her own. The only thing Kyle has left is the house he had built years ago before he had even ever met Mary. Most importantly though, he got the one thing that he wanted more than anything in this world, Mary is alive. He told Amanda once that if he had to do it again and give up everything he had to save her, he would. Now that is what true love is about: sacrifice, dedication, and hope.

If you are able to ask Mary today, is it faith that saved her life or medical technology, Mary would tell you it is faith. Think about what you have read. She died and came back, she couldn't even breathe on her own but then all of a sudden she could. When the doctors said she would never function on her own because a lot of her brain tissue was dead, she still beat the odds. She overcame everything that the doctors said she would not be able to.

Is it a miracle?
Yes, I believe it is.

The Heartache of a Child

When a baby is born it has no awareness of what its life will be like. It does not understand love or hate. It has no concept of joy or sorrow. It is not even aware of what the future holds for it. It is not until it starts to be self-aware that it starts to understand things. That is why it is so important for a parent to teach them so they grow and understand how the world works.

From the time we are born or sometimes even when we are not born, there is a purpose for everything. It could be that Father wants to change someone who is directly in contact with that life that he created. Sometimes it is to share something with others. Sometimes the talent that is given to someone in itself can become a message to the world. Father only shares what he wants to share only when he decides to share it. A good example of this is a songwriter. The song that is written whether the writer is aware of it or not comes from either an experience or being told something that Father wants them to share with others.

I think Amanda has more of a reason to hate Father (God) than anyone. Her childhood is not the way a normal one should be like. A child should have happiness and joy in their life. It should not know heartache at such a very young age. It should not feel alone or afraid of those who were supposed to protect her. She thinks Father must have hated her because he didn't protect her as he should have and she was angry about it. What she discovers, later on, is something she could never have realized or known. That her birth would mean more than what she thinks it ever could.

It all starts the moment her mother became ill. In order to understand compassion, you need someone close to you that is affected by something tragic, and for Amanda, it is her mother. She is more protective of her than anyone. The downside, however, is because of her mother's illness, Amanda had no choice but to grow up very quickly. It is her job to take over for her mother. She would clean the house and do the things a mother should be doing.

Childhood, for the most part, is not an option for her. Her dad tries to do what he could but there is only so much someone can do alone. He works sixteen hours a day just to keep up with the medical bills that are piling up. Amanda understands that what happened to her is not her parents' fault but she feels it is Father's (God's) fault. That is why she hated him. Now I will tell you her story and why she had a reason to. Here are the two questions to think about.

Do we suffer for no reason?
Or,
Does our suffering lead us closer to God?

CHAPTER 1

The Children's Home

It all starts with a knock on the door where a woman and a man take her away from her mother. They say she is not being taken care of by anyone the way she should have been. They also take her brother Jack with them. They take her to this children's home in another city. Amanda kicks and screams all the way to the place they were taking her and tells them that she needed to be with her mother. Amanda feels she needed to protect her mother and she did not want to go where they were taking her. The place she ended up at is cold, almost like the heater did not work. It is just about two weeks before Christmas. She complains about being cold but the people say, "Too bad, get used to it."

One of them tells Amanda, "You are lucky you have some place at all to stay at."

There are about eight children there, including her and her brother. That is probably the first time she feels hate where before she only felt love for others.

After about a week being there, she gets really ill. She has a fever and because it is so cold in the home it is probably what made her sick to begin with. On the day she is sick, they call her down for dinner and she came down to tell them that she did not feel like eating but they tell her they did not care and made her sit at the table anyways. Amanda, of course, starts crying and says she wanted her father.

One of the ladies pipes up and says, "Shut up and eat."

After about an hour, Amanda still did not eat her food. All the other children had got up and left because they ate, including her brother. Her brother did come back in about thirty minutes later to check on her but the lady would not let him walk into the room. He is told to go find something to do and stay out of it. Another hour has passed by and it is almost 8:00 p.m.

Amanda asks again if she could get up from the table and the mean lady says to her, "No! You are going to stay there all night until you eat."

Hours have passed and at around 11:00 p.m., Amanda is so tired she could barely keep her eyes open. Amanda finally starts picking and eating her food. The food has been sitting out now for at least five hours. She has peed her pants by then too because they didn't even let her get up to go to the bathroom. When she is finally allowed to get up, it is just about midnight at that point. When the lady saw she has peed her pants, she makes Amanda clean it up before she lets her go to her room.

The next day is no better. It starts off with Amanda being really tired since they woke her up at 5:00 a.m. Later on after dinner, they all go to bed. Amanda still has a fever and no one gave her anything for it. She is forced to eat even when she did not feel like it. Shortly after she goes to bed, she wakes up and vomits on the bed. The same mean lady is there. I think maybe she lives there. Amanda comes downstairs and tells her she had gotten sick in her bed.

Amanda says to her, "I got sick in my bed."

The lady says to her, "I don't care. Sleep in it."

Amanda gets so angry that she walks upstairs, gets the sheets off the bed, walks back down, throws them in the lady's face, and says to her, "You sleep in it."

The lady grabs Amanda, throws her to the ground, and starts kicking her while she lay there. Amanda tries to protect herself from the blows so she folds her arms and curls up into a ball. She gets kicked several times in the head, in the rib cage, and other places.

Amanda is crying and yelling, which woke another one of the children and he came downstairs and looks at her, and yells, and says, "Please stop."

The mean lady turns around and looks at the boy, slaps him right across the face, and says, "If you don't want some of this too go back to your room."

The boy leaves and did go back to his room.

Amanda finally yells out, "Father, please help me and make her stop."

Amanda was talking to God. Then all of a sudden, the lady stopped.

It is finally Christmas Eve and her father came to see her and brings her and her brother Christmas presents. The lady tells her father she could open them tomorrow. The lady never leaves her alone with her father so she could tell him what is going on. She would never even leave the room. Amanda wants so much to tell her father how she had been treated. Every time she would look over at the lady while her father is visiting her, the lady would run her hand across her throat as if to tell Amanda, "If you say anything, I will cut your throat." So Amanda keeps quiet about everything. Her father gives both her and her brother a hug and tell them both goodbye.

After her father had left, the lady takes her into another room and says to her, "You are lucky you kept your mouth shut." She then grabs the presents away from Amanda that her father had given to her and says, "You will get these back tomorrow." The one thing that Amanda could not understand is why she is so cruel to her but not to the other children there.

Christmas morning came and Amanda is one of the first children awake. She is so excited and could not wait to see what her father had bought her. After breakfast, they all go into a big room and she gets to open her presents, she is so happy about everything she was given. She got play dishes, she got an etch o sketch, even a big doll and a few other things. So being excited as children do on Christmas morning, she is singing and seems really happy.

Next thing Amanda knew is that she was snatched up from the floor and dragged into the hallway. She's standing in the hallway and there is the mean lady standing there looking at her.

Amanda says to her, "What did I do?"

The lady says, "You need to shut up. There are children here who don't have any presents." She then slams Amanda against the wall. She tells Amanda, "You stay here."

She comes back after a couple of minutes bringing Amanda's toys that her father gave her, then she stomps on them, breaking her etch o sketch, and she takes the doll and tears the legs and head off of it.

She hands Amanda the play dishes, which is all she had left, and the lady says, "Here, this is all you deserve."

Amanda then screams at her and says, "I hate you and I hate God too."

Amanda was raised to love God and to believe.

The lady comes back at her and says to her, "What kind of God could ever love a child like you?"

Amanda threw the dishes down and Amanda ran up to her room crying. Amanda stays in her room for quite a while. When Amanda finally came back downstairs, she sees a little blonde girl on the floor playing with the dishes her father had given her.

The little blonde girl says to Amanda, "Look at what I was given."

Amanda looks at her and says, "You can have them."

After that day, she hated Christmas but even when she was older and had children of her own, she never told her own children what had happened to her that cold Christmas Day. Every year she still buys them presents and plays Santa Claus but deep inside, more than anything in the world, she wishes she could have the presents back that her father had bought her that day and that none of it ever happened.

A few days later, Amanda wonders why the mean lady is not there at the home. Then she overhears one of the other adults say that she got into a car accident and was thrown through the windshield of the car and had died. Now you would think that Amanda would have been happy she is dead, but instead, Amanda gets down on her knees that night, starts crying, and she asks Father (God) to forgive her and take her to heaven with him. Despite what she was put through, she still wants to hope there is a God.

One night, lying in her room after the mean lady had died, one of the other ladies came in and starts talking to Amanda, now she is one of the nice ones.

She tells Amanda, "I am sorry for the way you were treated."

Amanda looks at her and says, "Why didn't you stop her?"

She says back to Amanda, "I was afraid of losing my job. I have a child of my own and need the money to take care of him."

Amanda looks at her and says, "Why did she hate me so much?"

So the nice lady says to her, "Well, a year ago her husband was driving down the road with her baby in the back seat of the car when a small child with dark hair and blue eyes like you had run out into the road. The husband tried to avoid hitting the little girl so he swerved and struck a pole that crushed the car and he and the baby died instantly."

Then Amanda remembers it was her that ran into the road that day. It was the day that she ran to the fire station across the street to get help because her mother's oxygen tanks ran out, and the alarms were going off, and her mother could not breathe. That is the day that her brother was at school and Sarah had run to the store and told Amanda she would be right back to keep an eye on her mother since her father was at work.

After the lady tells her that, she just starts crying.

Amanda says to her, "It was me. I didn't mean to hurt them. I was just trying to save my mother's life that day."

It was not until that moment that Amanda realized why the lady hated her so much and did the things that she did to her. The thing about life is that every single thing that happens is a chain reaction to something else and for some reason, Father (God) only knows why it happens.

It was about a month later that her father gets her and her brother back home after going to court. The judge had talked to the children and Amanda is able to finally tell someone what had happened to her, and she only told it to the judge behind closed doors. Two weeks later, they close the children's home for good.

Amanda never did tell her father what happened to her in the children's home that day. Sadly enough that was just the beginning of the pain that Amanda would suffer through her life.

CHAPTER 2

Alone

Amanda is nine years old now and things really have not changed much. She still struggles trying to do the right thing for her mother. One day, her aunt Amanda shows up with another woman. Now Amanda did not know her aunt very well. She had maybe seen her once before this. She knew she was named after her aunt but that is really all she knew about her.

Her aunt says to her, "I am your Aunt Amanda and you have to come with me."

Little Amanda says to her, "I am not going anywhere with you. I need to stay and take care of my mother."

Her aunt Amanda says to her, "You don't have a choice." She then snatches Amanda up and drags her to the car crying and kicking, while the other lady grabs her brother. She cries during the whole trip, up until they arrived to where she is being taken to, which is Michigan.

When Kyle came home later that night he asks Sarah, "Where are the children?"

Sarah responds and says, "Your wife's sister was here with a lady from DCFS and took them."

Kyle says, "Not again! Why can't these people stay out of our lives? The children are well taken care of. There is no reason for any of this."

He gets on the phone and starts making some phone calls. He finds out that Aunt Amanda had taken them to Michigan with her. He is so upset over everything that he knew what he would have to go through again to get his children back.

The next day, when Amanda and her brother arrive at her aunt's house in Michigan, Aunt Amanda shows them where they are going to be sleeping. It is not a very big house. Amanda's room is in the basement. Amanda hates cold places, it reminds her of what happened last time. They have no running water, just well water, and there is an outhouse when you have to go to the bathroom. Amanda is thinking that her parents' home is a lot nicer than this. Aunt Amanda's home has two bedrooms where her home had, at one time, six bedrooms. They put Jack in one of the bedrooms but stuck her in the basement and she could not understand why.

The next day she is taken to register for school there. They start going to school there the following Monday. Amanda hates the fact that she didn't know anyone there. She feels so lonely and she is so afraid that no one would like her; all children have that fear when something happens that changes their life. Of course, sometimes adults can have that same fear too. Change is always a hard thing to deal with.

The night before the first day of school, her aunt calls her upstairs and says, "Amanda, sit down here. I am going to cut your hair."

Amanda says to her, "I don't want my hair cut." Amanda has the most beautiful dark brown hair that is really long, almost to her butt. She hardly ever lets anyone touch it. So the whole time her aunt is cutting her hair, all she is doing was crying. To make matters worse, her aunt puts curlers in her hair afterward and makes her sleep on them. She barely gets any sleep at all. She cries practically all night to the point where the next morning she has swelling under her eyes.

There is at least one person that she is able to become friends with while she is there and she has horses. That was the first time in her life that Amanda rode a horse, never with a saddle and reins though but bareback. She had so much fun doing so too.

A week later after being there, her brother Jack gets really ill. He starts running a fever and has severe pain in his side. Finally, her aunt takes him to the hospital and it turns out his appendix had burst. He is in the hospital for quite a long time. Amanda, of course, was alone with her aunt and her uncle. Now her uncle is okay, she just hardly ever talks to him.

Just when Amanda thinks things couldn't get worse, they did. She starts feeling like Cinderella, like the only reason her aunt took her from her mother is to make her a slave. She would sit by herself at night and wish that someone would come to save her. She barely even gets to speak to her father at all and that is very disheartening to her.

More than anything in this world, she is so worried about her mom. Every time she has a chance to even speak to her dad she would ask him how her mother is doing. She misses her mom more than anything in this world. All she wants to do is protect her and watch over her. When she was at home, Amanda would always make a point to go into her mother's room and read her stories and say prayers by her bed. Amanda wishes more than anything in the world that her mother would come back to her.

She is forced to stay at her aunt's house for three months. Finally, her father is able to take her and her brother home again. She is so happy to see her mother again. At this point, Mary is doing a lot better than the last time Amanda had seen her mother. She would sit up in bed and she could actually talk to her without slurring her words as much as she had before Amanda was taken.

I wish I could tell you that there is a happy ending to Amanda's childhood but unfortunately for little Amanda, there wasn't and what happened next would change Amanda's life forever and make her hate Father (God) so much.

CHAPTER 3

Innocence

Amanda just turned eleven years old when her father asks her if she would like to go see her grandpa in Washington State. Amanda is like, "I would love to see my grandpa."

Amanda asks, "Well does that mean I can stay there for a while with my grandpa and grandma?"

Her dad Kyle answers and says, "Yeah, if that is what you and your brother would like to do."

She always has so much fun with her grandpa and grandma when she gets to see them. They played cards with her, and went fishing, and camping, and all kinds of fun things. One thing she remembered the most was the one time that he went hunting and killed a deer inside a park, which was not allowed. Well, the deer was not the size that was allowed to be killed anyways and because of where they were at, at that time if he would have been caught he would have gotten into trouble. Amanda remembered that her grandfather got this idea to put her into the bathroom of the camper so when he went out the gates for inspection then she could say she was in there using it. So he took this deer and sat it on the toilet and then put Amanda in the bathroom with it. When the park ranger came into the camper to look around and started to open the door to the bathroom, Amanda yelled out, "I am in here." On the way out of the park, Amanda's grandpa hit a bump pinning her against the door because of the deer. So Amanda looked at this dead deer in her face. When they finally got back to grandpa's house, he decided he was going to gut it. And, of course, he decided that he wanted Amanda to help. So he put the knife in Amanda's hand and pulled down with it, cutting the deer wide open. After that, she never ate deer meat again. In a way, it kind of traumatized her.

Amanda, however, learned a lot of other things from him during the time she was there with him. Stick fishing and how to tell which direction she was walking if ever she gets lost in the woods. Amanda could never tell north, south, east, or west, but if you were to show her a tree, she could tell which way she was going only because of how trees grow according to when the sun hits them.

It has been about two weeks now since Amanda had arrived in Washington state. Her grandpa and grandma have to go somewhere so grandpa asks if his stepson Tim would be willing to take the children in for a few weeks. The step-uncle Tim and aunt Josephine did take the children in, it was convenient because they did live in the same city that Amanda's grandpa and grandma lived in.

At first, everything is okay. Amanda gets to watch her uncle operate a bridge for barges and she makes a new friend down the street. Amanda and her new friend love the new music that came out. It is the beginning of the disco era. Amanda and her new friend have a really good time together. Everything is going well until one day her aunt takes her brother shopping.

Amanda had walked home from her friend's house to find her uncle there alone. She walks into the house as she had done before and she says to her uncle, "Hi, where is Aunt Josephine and Jack at?"

Her uncle responds back and says, "I sent them to the store."

Amanda replies, "Oh, okay."

Then her uncle Tim says, "Will you help me in my bedroom for a minute, I dropped something and I cannot reach it."

Amanda tells him, "Sure, I can do that."

They walk into the bedroom and as Amanda is getting ready to bend down and look under the bed, her uncle grabs her. He throws her on the bed and rapes her. Her uncle is very drunk. Now I am not going to go into detail about what happened to her but let's just say it changed Amanda's view of men forever. It is very hard for her to trust any man after that.

Once he was done, he gets up and says to her, "Don't tell anyone or I promise you, you will never see your mom again."

Unfortunately, Amanda believes him.

It was about an hour later that her aunt came home with her brother. When they get there, Amanda is in her room crying.

Her aunt says to her husband, "Where is Amanda at?"

Her husband answers and says, "She is in her room I think."

Her aunt walks in and sees Amanda crying and says to her, "What's wrong?"

Amanda answers her and says, "I hit my head on the dresser."

This, of course, is a lie.

Her aunt says to her, "Let me take a look at it."

Amanda replies, "No, it's okay, it was just a slight bump."

When dinner came, Amanda asks her aunt if she could just eat in her room. She tells her it is because she just wants to do something different. Her aunt lets her. The true reason is that she did not want to see her uncle or even look at him after what he had done to her. Amanda wishes she would never have to come out of that room again.

The next morning, when Amanda gets up, there is blood all over the bed where she is lying. Amanda freaks out because she has no idea that it was there for.

Amanda yells out, "Aunt Josephine, something is wrong."

Her uncle had already left for work by this time.

Her aunt walks into the room and says, "What is wrong, honey?"

Amanda answers her, pulls back the blanket, and says to her, "Look, something is wrong with me." She still did not tell her aunt what had happened to her.

Her aunt responds and says, "Oh, that is normal. You are having a period."

Her aunt then sits next to her and explains everything to her. After everything is explained to Amanda, Amanda then understands why it could have happened now. She still does not say one word, though, about what happened. She thinks she would be blamed or that her uncle would hurt her.

CHAPTER 4

Scared

Two weeks pass and she could not even look at her uncle or even talk to him. She would not even look him in the eyes. She is so riddled with guilt for what he had done to her. It takes a very long time before she would look another man in the eyes and to this day she has a problem doing that when it comes to men she does not know.

Then one day, she wakes up early in the morning and she comes out to the front room and she sees her uncle sitting on the couch, so she starts to walk back to her room where she feels safe.

Her uncle speaks up and says to her, "Your aunt and brother should be up at any time. Why don't you come over here and sit next to me on the couch."

Amanda answers him and says, "No, thank you."

Her uncle then says to her, "Come here now." So because she is scared of him, she does what she is told to do and sits down beside him.

While sitting there trying to stay as far as she can from him, he says to her, "Come closer and sit next to me."

Amanda says back to him, "I am fine sitting where I am at."

Then her uncle Tim says, "Now, Amanda. Do what you are told."

So she scoots closer to him as she was told to do, but she is scared to be that close to him. While sitting there, she is nervous and she just wants to crawl out of her skin and run into another room. Next thing she knew her uncle starts putting his hands between her legs and she yells out, "*No!*"

Then her aunt walks into the room and says, "No what, Amanda?"

"Nothing, Aunt Josephine," she says back to her.

Her aunt then walks into the kitchen to get a cup of coffee.

While her aunt is in the kitchen, her uncle says to her, "I will get you alone later, you just wait and see." That is when Amanda jumps up and goes running to her room.

That afternoon came and Tim says to Josephine, "Why don't you take Jack shopping for some new clothes?"

Aunt Josephine responds and says, "Why don't I take both the children with me?"

Then, Uncle Tim says, "That is not a good idea. You would have your hands full with both of them. Amanda can stay here with me."

Josephine replies back and says, "Yeah, I guess you are right, it might be a good idea to take them one at a time."

When Amanda hears her uncle talking to her aunt she came back out of her room. Josephine says to her, "Amanda, I am going to take Jack shopping with me and I will be back later. I will take you shopping tomorrow okay?"

Amanda speaks up and says, "Please, Aunt Josephine, take me too."

Josephine responds and says, "I promise I will take you tomorrow," and then her aunt and brother leave.

Right after they walk out, she goes into her room and hides under the bed. She is hoping her uncle could not find her. She is scared to death what he might do to her. He did, however, find her and drag her out from under the bed. He then throws her on the bed and sits down beside her. She kicks and yells at him.

He slaps her, puts his hand over her mouth, and says, "You can make this easy or you can make this hard." He then pulls down his pants and says, "You will rub him."

She tries to kick him again and run away but he is so much stronger than she is. He then slaps her in the face and says, "Do what you are told."

Then as this was going on, he starts to remove Amanda's clothes from her when someone knocks at the door. He tells Amanda, "Don't you move."

Then she hears her grandpa's voice, she gets her clothes back on and she goes running out to him. The moment she sees him, she says, "Grandpa."

Grandpa picks her up and says to her, "How is my little sunshine doing today?"

Amanda says, "I am okay. Can I leave with you please?"

Grandpa answers and says, "Of course, you can come with me. Grandma and I are back so you guys can come back to the house now."

Her uncle then proceeds to look at her like he could kill her.

Then her grandpa says, "By the way, where is Aunt Josephine and Jack at?"

Uncle Tim responds and says, "They went shopping."

Amanda being curious asks him, "Why did you leave us?"

Grandpa just responds and says, "Your aunt Amanda was very ill and we wanted to make sure we were there for her."

Amanda says to him, "Is my Aunt Amanda okay?"

Grandpa responds back and says, "No, I am sorry she passed away."

Amanda thinks, *This is the aunt a couple years earlier that took her away from her mother and father.*

Uncle Tim then pipes up and says to his stepfather, "Can I talk to Amanda for a minute before you take her with you?"

Grandpa says, "Of course you can."

He takes Amanda into another room where Grandpa could not hear them, squeezes her face, and says to her, "You say one thing and you will be blamed for what happened between us and I will hurt everyone you care about, including your grandpa."

Amanda and Tim walk back into the room Grandpa is standing in and Grandpa says, "So, you ready to go, sunshine? Hey, by the way where did you get that bruise on your face?"

Amanda stands there and trying to think what to tell him when her uncle says, "The swing came back and hit her in the face this morning."

Grandpa says to her, "Are you okay, sunshine?"

Amanda answers him back and says, "Yes, Grandpa, can we go now please?" Amanda just wants to get out there as fast as she could and away from her uncle.

Amanda and her grandpa finally leave and while in the car her grandpa says to her, "Are you okay? You're being awfully quiet more than usual?"

She answers him back and says, "I am now that I am with you, Grandpa." Then Grandpa looks at her with this curious look on his face like he knew there was something she is not telling him.

When she gets to Grandpa's house, she asks him, "Can I go back home to Mommy and Daddy now?"

Grandpa replies, "Is this what you would like to do, sunshine?"

Amanda replies, "Yes, please."

Grandpa then says, "Well, let me call your father, see how things are going, and see if everything is okay with your mother first."

So her grandpa makes the call and lets Amanda's father know that Amanda wants to come home. Then Kyle asks, "Does Jack want to come home too?"

Grandpa responds, "I am not sure. I will have to call and ask him, he is still over at Tim and Josephine's house."

Kyle says, "Well, call them and find out, but yes the children can come home if they want too." Then Kyle hangs up the phone.

So after talking to Kyle, Grandpa calls his stepson's house and says, "Amanda is going back home to Illinois would Jack like to go too?" You could hear Tim talking to Jack and you could hear Jack in the background saying, "No, I want to stay here longer."

The next day, Amanda gets on a plane to head back home to Illinois. When her father picks her up at the airport, she is so happy to see him and to be home again. On the drive back, Amanda's dad asks her, "Did you enjoy spending time there?"

Amanda just replies, "I loved spending time with grandma and grandpa." She didn't say one word however about her uncle or her aunt.

All Amanda tries to do over the next few weeks is to try and block out what her uncle had done to her. It is more than she could bear. She keeps having reoccurring nightmares of what had happened to her and remembering her uncle's voice and the pain she felt.

CHAPTER 5

Wanting to Die

It is a beautiful day and the sun is shining outside but inside Amanda is crying. Amanda never did tell her mother or father, and not even her grandpa and grandma, what had happened to her in Washington. Instead, Amanda let it tear her up inside. Then one day her father had to take her mother to the doctor's office and Amanda's father asks her if she wants to go and Amanda just tells him no.

After her parents leave, Amanda makes the decision that she just doesn't want to live any longer with the pain she feels inside. The shame and guilt that she feels over what had happened to her are more than she could bear any more.

She decides it is time to say goodbye to the world that she looked at as being cruel and heartless. She also wonders what kind of God would make a child suffer so much in just such a few short years of her life.

She leaves a couple of letters behind, one addressed to her older brother whom she felt had abandoned her when she needed him the most and one to her mother and father. She goes into the medicine cabinet and she grabs her mother's medicine that is in it. Then she goes into the kitchen and gets beer out of the refrigerator.

She knows that her mother and father would not be back for a few hours so she had plenty of time to end it. After what happened to her, she asked her dad to put a lock on the inside of her bedroom door so she could hook it when she gets scared. Her father never asked her why all of sudden she wanted a lock; I guess he just assumed she is at that age where she wanted privacy.

She takes the medicine and the beer, goes back into her room, and barricades herself in it. She locks the door and even puts the dresser behind the door, hoping no one could open it. She then locks the windows to her bedroom so they could not be opened from the outside.

She sits down on her bed and cries while she is writing her letters. She does not tell them why she is killing herself but what she had felt for them and that she would miss them dearly but not to blame themselves for her decision. It is her choice and her choice alone to make. While the letters are being written she is drinking the beer and taking the bottle of pills. There must have been at least twenty pills in the bottle and she probably drank three beers during this time.

As Amanda lies there dying and getting to the point where she is having trouble breathing, she hears a voice say, "Not yet, my child." What she could not understand is there was no one in the house but her. A few more minutes passed and the last thing she hears is glass breaking just before she stopped breathing altogether.

She wakes up in the hospital a few days later and asks her dad, "Who saved me?"

Her dad looks at her and says, "A man came by the house and broke the bedroom window and pulled you out of the room."

Then Amanda says to him, "But how did he know I was there?"

Her dad says to her, "He said he heard what sounded like a moaning sound when he got out of his vehicle in the driveway."

Amanda's room is right next to the driveway so she thinks that is possible. She doesn't really remember much after feeling like she could not breathe except the voice she heard. She wonders who could have it been that really saved her that day.

Her dad Kyle asks her, "Why did you try and kill yourself? I don't understand what would make you do something like that and your letters didn't say why but that you thought God hated you."

Amanda just says, "I don't want to talk about it please, Dad. I shouldn't even be here still."

Kyle says to her, "You almost weren't. Your heart had stopped and they had to bring you back."

Amanda looks up at him and says, "I love you. It is not your fault just so you know."

After that, a couple of nurses come into the ICU unit and say that Amanda needs her rest. They ask her father to go for a while and let her sleep, and so he does. Then they check Amanda's IV, and shortly after she falls asleep.

Amanda stays in the hospital over the course of the next three days. Then finally, after talking to a counselor, they let her go home. She still does not tell anyone, even the counselor, why she did it.

Just around a week later, as Amanda is falling asleep she remembered something and it is something she would never forget again after that night. She doesn't remember exactly everything, but there is one thing she does remember when she died. It was like a dream, but she knows it wasn't.

She remembers being in a field of grass and how beautiful it had looked. She could smell it and she could also smell the flowering trees that she could see as she is walking. Then she had this smell, like something is burning. She walks up a hill and hears a voice say, "Come, child, take my hand." As she takes their hand and continues to walk up the hill, she sees two burning bushes in front of her.

Amanda says, "What is this?"

Then she hears the voice say, "Choose."

Amanda stands there by the burning bushes; even though they looked like they were on fire, there is no heat coming from them. She then says, "Where am I?"

The voice answers and says, "You are neither here nor there but you are what you consider to be between heaven and earth."

Amanda, at this point, is completely confused.

So then Amanda says, "Choose what?"

The voice then says, "Look into the bushes. Here is a bush with all the riches in the world and the other one has nothing but a book, now you must choose. One choice will come with great suffering and the other will bring you great riches."

Amanda did not know what to think of what is happening to her or why it is happening. She thinks maybe she is dreaming or something. Amanda looks at all the shiny things that are in the one bush and then looks at the old book in the other and she sees that it says "The Book of Life." So she reaches her hand into the fire with the book and she pulls it out of the fire. The book is very worn and old but for some reason, she is drawn to it.

Then she hears the voice saying, "With this book you will know great suffering but also I will give you the knowledge that I have not yet told the world. The suffering will not last forever I promise but without it, I will not be able to show you the things I need you to know and to share with my children."

Then, all of a sudden, the voice says to her, "I am now sending you back with a message for my children. You will not remember the message until later on in life when I tell you it is time to remember. Then I want you to promise me you will share it with them. Can you do that for me?"

Amanda says, "Yes, but who are you?"

The voice says, "I am he. I am the one who the world has forgotten. The one they will turn away from someday."

Then, all of a sudden, Amanda hears a voice say, "Go back, my child."

Next thing she knew, she opens her eyes and there are a lot of people around her. She hears a voice say, "You're awake."

Amanda thinks it is strange she remembers the dream or what she thinks was a dream she had but she did not remember the message she was given. It is not until she came to be an adult that she would remember the message she was told to share and the other things she was shown.

Just a few days after dying, she starts having dreams. Dreams like no other, and every time she awakens she remembers them as if she is actually standing there watching it happen right in front of her. She would remember every detail except one thing—she doesn't know where the event is taking place or when it is going to take place, but she somehow knows it would.

The one day out of the blue, she has a dream, and on that day, she remembers the message she was given the day she died. Then she realized she is not like anyone else.

She has suffered greatly in her life and thinks the pain would never stop. Every time she is hurt by someone or something such as death, it is not just that hurt or that death she feels but all the pain from everything she ever feels from everything that has happened since birth would come back all at once.

Amanda's suffering ends up not being for nothing.

There ends up being a reason for it all.

Common Destiny

Do you believe in destiny? Could it be possible that two people are supposed to meet each other? What if you were told that there is a person out there that you were meant to meet? Would you believe it?

The woman in this story thinks that God didn't care about her and so she lost her faith in him. Then one day, she is given a message about a man she would meet. She is told that through this man she would learn to love again, and through that love, her faith would be restored. So here are the questions you must ask yourself.

Is it God that wants them to meet to help restore
   her faith?
Or
Is it her love for this man that restores her faith
   in God?

CHAPTER 1

Amanda's First Message

It is summertime, and just about everyone likes summer. The sun is hot; you can cook out, have picnics, go camping, swimming, and just enjoy the weather. You think, *What a nice time of year.* I want you to meet someone. She has dark hair, blue eyes, and looks kind of like her mother. Her name is Amanda. That's right, Mary's daughter.

Amanda's all grown-up now. She's married and has two children of her own. Amanda's not happy with her life right now. She loves her children very much, but Amanda feels she got married too soon. Amanda was pregnant at the time and felt she had no choice. She cares about her husband, but he is always mean to her. He puts her down, makes fun of her, uses her, lies to her, cheats on her, and even sometimes steals from her. Amanda knows in her heart that she isn't loved or he would not treat her that way.

Amanda's always felt that because of having no childhood like normal children do, having to grow up too fast, getting married too soon, and being treated so badly that God didn't love her, she lost her faith in him. Amanda thinks she never would know what love truly meant. So she became cold in her heart. She never would let anybody get too close to her. Then one day her mother calls her and says she wants to talk to her. So Amanda tells her mother she would come and see her. Now Amanda has no clue what it was that her mother wants.

It's July 7, 1994. Amanda had just got off of work. She is tired and a little crabby. The phone rings and Amanda picks it up.

"Hello."

"Hi, Amanda, can you come by and see me today?" Mary says to her.

"I don't know, Mom. I am a little tired. I really don't feel like going anywhere," Amanda explains.

"Please, Amanda, I have something important to tell you," Mary says to her.

Amanda replies to her mother, saying, "Okay, Mom, if it's that important to you. I'll come by in a few minutes, but I can't stay very long. I have to make Tom and the children dinner."

Mary says, "That's fine. I'll see you in a few minutes."

Amanda's mother only lives a block and a half away from her house, so Amanda drives down there. When she pulls up outside, she sees Mary sitting on the picnic table that Amanda's father made for her as a child.

Amanda walks over to her mother and says to her, "What do you want?"

"Please sit down."

So Amanda did what her mother wanted her to do.

"Okay, Mom, what was so important that I had to see you today?"

"You're going to change jobs in a few weeks and when you do, you're going to meet a man that is going to be very important to you."

Amanda says to her mother, "What kind of nonsense are you talking about?" Amanda never believes anything her mother says because she knew her mother was mentally ill. She would confuse things and sometimes say things Amanda didn't understand.

Amanda just looks at her mom and says, "I'm leaving. I have things to do."

"Please, Amanda, stay. I have more to tell you."

Amanda wouldn't listen to her mother. She gets up and leaves, anyway. Mary realizes there is no love in her daughter's heart.

A few weeks later, Amanda finds out that she's getting ready to be laid off from work. The grocery store she worked at is going out of business. So Amanda starts looking for another job. She is finally able to find one, but she would not be able to start working until July 29. It is a little convenience store on campus. The person who is working there is getting ready to quit. Amanda's new job is going to be making sandwiches and running the cash register. Amanda really didn't care what she does for a living. She just wants to feel she belongs somewhere.

Then on July 29, 1994, it is Amanda's first day on the job. It seems that everybody at work is nice to her. They say hi to her and ask her what her name is. She thinks this is okay. Amanda thinks, *I'm going to like it here.*

However, she does feel a little nervous. When Amanda has changes in her life, it always makes her nervous. She never lets other people see this, but inside she is scared, especially when it comes to men. She has always been afraid to say the wrong thing. That maybe they would not like her or that they may think she is too serious. It's not that she tries to be serious, but it is just her way sometimes of shutting people out, kind of like a defense mechanism. When she acts like herself, she feels that she's making herself vulnerable to others.

Amanda knows better than to let anyone get too close to her. The way her husband treats her, she feels that they would probably treat her the same way he does. Amanda thinks that all men are cruel. She thinks that they all played games too much; none of them wish to speak about what they feel. On the outside, they usually keep this wall in front of them. Amanda feels that a man's greatest fear is to let a woman really get too close to them. Some men believe that if you get too close to them that it makes them less than a man, but that's not true because in reality it makes them a better man than they were before.

Amanda has always thought that her father Kyle is the perfect man. On the outside, he is tough and rugged like a man should be. On the inside, he is kind and gentle. He never raised his voice at Mary, he never lied to her and he never kept secrets from her. When he would have a bad day at work, he would tell her how he felt.

When some pretty girl would flirt with him, he would tell her. In every aspect of his life, he never kept her in the dark. He loved Mary enough to share everything with her. More importantly, he loved her enough to give his life for hers if he had to. Amanda always thought what her father did for her mother is what true love is about.

Over the next two weeks, Amanda really gets to know the people that came into the store. She learns most of their names. Amanda tries to be really outgoing so she can try and hide the hurt and pain inside. So she would kid and joke with them when they came in. There is one set of guys that seem to come in there every day. They work doing the same thing, but they seem to be in pairs like partners. One of them, Amanda thinks, is really cute. She doesn't know his name, so she doesn't say too much to him at first. She is afraid to say the wrong thing.

Then on August 3, 1994, Amanda's mom calls her again and says they need to talk. So Amanda tells her mother she would come and see her in a little while. Amanda thinks, *What could she possibly want now?* So when Amanda leaves work, she stops by her parents' house to see what it is that her mother wants.

When Amanda gets to the house, she walks in and Mary is standing there singing and doing dishes. Amanda always thought her mother had the most beautiful voice she had ever heard. Even though Amanda was so little then, she remembers her mother singing her to sleep.

"Hi, Mom, what did you want to talk to me about?" Amanda says.

Mary replies, "Hold on a minute, let me finish washing these dishes."

Amanda stands there waiting for her mother to finish.

"Okay, I'm done. Let's go outside and talk."

"That's fine with me," Amanda says with curiosity in her voice.

When they are both outside, they sit down on the picnic table.

"So, Mom, what did you want?"

"I have something to tell you, and you must try and understand. It is very important." Mary is being very serious at this point.

"Wait a minute, Mom. First, tell me how you knew I was going to change jobs?" Amanda wants to know how she knew what she knew.

"Just listen to me and I'll explain everything," her mom says to her with a certain tone in her voice.

"All right, I'm listening." Amanda rolls her eyes at that point.

"Do you remember when I died that day back in 1970 and I came back to life? I want to tell you what happened to me. First I saw this bright light, at the end of this light, was a place I had never seen before. It had a big fence around it, which looked like gold. A man came up to me, took my hand, and said he had something he wanted to show me. He then took me through the gate. On the inside of the gate, there were trees and houses just like here on earth. It was the most beautiful place I had ever seen. The ground was like a sheet of glass."

Amanda looks at her and says, "What are you talking about?"

Mary doesn't answer Amanda but instead continues talking.

"When I was walking with him, he said he had something else to show me. He put me in a dark place like a prison. There were people in there that were gnashing at their teeth just as the Bible says. There was no way out and I was very scared. Then all of sudden he grabbed my hand again and pulled me out of that place. Then he says to me, 'Do you know why I showed you this?' I told him, 'No, I didn't understand.' Then he says, 'I am sending you back so you may live and deliver three messages for me when I tell you it is time to. I want you to give it to the person I tell you to.' He tells me who the messages were to be told to. Then he asks me if I understood and I said yes," Mary explains.

Amanda interrupts her and says, "What does any of this have to do with me?"

Mary looks at Amanda and says, "The messages are for you."

"You're crazy. I never heard such a thing in my life. Maybe everybody is right about you. You really are off your rocker."

"Please, Amanda, it is important. Listen to me and I'll explain everything."

"Why should I? You are not making any sense. I'll go ahead and listen to you but I still say this is crazy." She has no idea about what her mother is trying to say to her.

"The man that took my hand was the same man that told me to give you this message," Mary tries to explain it to her, 'I know you think that I forgot about you and that I don't love you because of everything you have been through. So I will show you I do love you and I am real. Therefore, in the end, you will believe in me and tell the world about me and you will remember the message I gave to you as a child to share with the world.'"

"Mom, what is going on? Have you lost your mind?" Amanda, at this point, is so overwhelmed that she almost thought it isn't her mother talking to her anymore. When she heard the message it wasn't even her mother's voice who said it. The voice that came from her mother was a voice though that she has heard before, but she did not understand where she had heard it.

Her mother responds, "I am just telling you what I was told to tell you." Then her mom's voice seemed normal again.

"Look, I have to leave," Amanda gets up, says goodbye to her mother, and leaves. Amanda refuses to believe anything she just heard her mother tell her.

CHAPTER 2

The Second Message

September 6, 1994. Amanda's at work and she's working really hard. Finally, it is quiet and she is able to take it easy for a few minutes. Then in walks the group of guys that are always together. She finally decides it is time to ask them their names.

When they get to the register, she says to them, "What are your names?"

One of them speaks up and says, "I'm Bill, this is Mack, and over there is Ralph." They all start kidding around with Amanda.

Bill says to her, "Did you know that Ryan talks about you all of the time?"

"Who's Ryan?" Amanda asks with curiosity in her voice.

"The one that has dark hair that is usually with us," Bill says with this smile on his face like he was the cat that swallowed the canary.

"Yeah, sure he does," Amanda thinks, *I wonder if that is the cute one.*

They all stand around for a few minutes joking and laughing and then they leave. A while later, she did find out that it was the cute one they were talking about.

On one of the days that Ryan and Mack came in, one of them say something to the fact that Ryan wasn't married. Later on, Amanda finds out that he is married. Amanda and Ryan starts talking more every day.

Then on October 1, 1994, Amanda's mother calls her again.

"Hi, Amanda, have you thought about what I said? You haven't come to see me or talk to me in almost a month."

"Yes, Mom. I remember what you said to me," Amanda answers her a little annoyed about it.

"There is still more I have to tell you. Will you come by and let me tell you the rest?" Mary is hoping that Amanda would.

Amanda says, "Okay, if it will make you happy. I'll listen to what you have to say."

Amanda goes down to her mother again, and this time they sit in the car to talk.

"All right, Mom, what else were you supposed to tell me?"

"This is the second message I was supposed to tell you. You will meet a man that you will soon come to love, and because of that love you are willing to leave him and give your life for his and in the end, you will believe again."

Amanda, still not believing, says, "Yeah and I suppose you know what he looks like."

"I do have visions of him sometimes. So yes I can tell you about him." Mary is being very serious even though she knows Amanda didn't believe her.

"Well, if you know so much let me hear some more about him." Amanda thinks her mother is still mentally ill, so she never takes anything she says to heart.

Mary looks at Amanda and tells her this, "Here is what I am supposed to tell you about him. He has dark wavy hair, blue eyes, he's taller than you, older than you, he has an important job, and he makes good money. You already know him and he's a Christian. That is all I am supposed to tell you for now except that you will be seeing him not only at work but other places too."

"All right, Mom, I have to leave now."

Amanda starts the car. Mary gets out of the car so Amanda could go home. When she did, she says to her, "I know you don't believe me now, but someday you will know I am telling you the truth."

It's October 11, 1994. Amanda knows Halloween is coming soon so she thinks she had better stop by K-Mart and get the children costumes and candy. She's standing in the checkout lane when she sees the shy cute one from work walk in. Amanda doesn't say hi to him because she doesn't know what to say. Amanda is always outgoing, but when it came to someone she likes, she has a hard time saying anything to them. Besides, Amanda doesn't feel she knows him well enough.

The next day at work, the guys come into the store again.

Amanda looks at them, smiles, and says, "Hi, brats."

After they were standing there talking for a moment, the cute one finally walks in. He gets what he wants and then walks over to the cash register.

Amanda looks at him and says, "I saw you yesterday at K-Mart."

"You saw me at K-Mart? Why didn't you say hi?" Ryan is smiling when he says it.

"Well, I didn't know if you were alone or not so I thought it would be better if I didn't say anything to you." So Amanda finished ringing him up and they leave.

It's Christmas 1994, and Amanda's parents came over to the house to eat with them. While Kyle is sitting in the living room with Tom, Amanda is standing in the kitchen with Mary talking and making Christmas dinner like she has done every year for her family.

Mary looks at Amanda and just had to say something to her. She says, "So Amanda, do you know who it is yet?"

"It's Christmas day. You're not going to start talking about that again, I hope." Amanda could not understand why her mother would not drop this.

"I am just curious if you had any clues of who it is." Mary is being very persistent. Amanda's mom tries to talk to her the whole time she is there. Amanda finally convinces her mom that she doesn't want to talk about it right now, especially knowing Tom is in the next room.

When her parents finally leave, Tom looks at Amanda and says to her, "What were you and your mom talking about in the kitchen?"

Amanda answers him and says, "You know my mom, she was just acting strangely."

Amanda didn't want Tom to know about what Mary has been telling her. She knows that Tom would forbid her from seeing her mother.

Six months had passed since Christmas. By this time, Amanda knows everybody's name at work. She thinks that they are a great bunch of people. She became good friends with all of them, especially the cute one.

It's Saturday, June 10, 1995. Amanda decides she wants to go and see a movie. Tom hardly ever lets her go anywhere without him and the children going with her. So they go with her. She wants to go see *Congo*. When she gets to the theater, she finds out that *Congo* is sold out. So they decide to stay and watch *Die Hard with a Vengeance* instead.

When she gets into the theater, she realizes that the lady at the counter didn't put butter on the popcorn. So she walks back up to the counter to get some and she has this strange feeling come over her. As she's standing at the counter, she looks up and sees Ryan standing right across from her on the other side. She smiles at him once she sees him but then realizes that he might not be alone. So she thinks it best not to say anything.

When she gets back in her seat, she realizes that he could walk into the same theater she is in. Through the whole movie, Amanda feels uneasy. Tom keeps asking her what is wrong, but she keeps saying nothing. She starts thinking about what her mother had told her and she wonders if it could be him that her mother's been telling her about. Amanda thinks how that could be since her mother's mentally ill. I mean if you think about it, Mary did have brain damage due to the coma and all. Amanda thinks that maybe it is just a coincidence running into him twice not being at work.

The following Monday at work when Mack and Ryan came into the store, Amanda decides she would tease Ryan about seeing him at the theater.

"What are you doing watching a movie with me?" she says with a smile on her face and laughing.

He says, "Not me!" Then he just kind of smiles back at her.

Amanda walks over to the magazine rack to put some magazines away. Ryan comes over to where she was at and grabs a newspaper. When he bends down to pick it up, he says to her, "How did you get such blue eyes with such dark hair?"

Amanda answers him and says, "That's because I have Indian and German in me."

He says to her, "Well that explains it."

Right about then Amanda's boss yells at her and says, "It would be nice to get some help over here."

She is always snapping and yelling at Amanda. Amanda couldn't understand why she is so bitter. Amanda later realizes it is because of all the heartaches she had been through. The way the owners treat her wasn't good too. Otherwise, Amanda thinks she is a nice person. Just so you know, Amanda's boss is her mother-in-law. Amanda thinks Mondays are the worst days of the week, and she is glad when they are over.

Over the next few weeks, Amanda goes to work like she always did. Every day she gets closer and closer to Ryan. They talk more and more every day. After a while, Amanda thinks he is different from others she has met, that there is something about him she just cannot shake. It is just a feeling she has when she is around him, like she feels safe and that he will not let anyone hurt her. They are becoming really good friends, at least she thinks so. Amanda still doesn't know if this is the man her mother told her about.

It's July 7, 1995. Amanda finds out today at work that her mother-in-law is leaving the company and she isn't going to be a manager anymore. Amanda is hoping that this is best for her, maybe it would make her happy again. Today she also gets to see Ryan and Mack. Amanda is busy filling the fountain machine with ice, while Ryan was getting a drink.

Amanda could not resist saying something smart to him. "You better leave; we don't allow dogs in here."

Ryan replies to Amanda, "You would miss me if I was gone."

Amanda says to him, "No, I won't."

Ryan says, "Yes, you will."

It is not until that moment that she realizes she does feel something for him.

Over the next few weeks, the company makes Amanda the temporary manager. They say she is on a trial basis until February of next year. She has to prove to them that she can do the job. Then they will make her the new manager of the store. That seems to be very important to Amanda because then she can always be where Ryan is at. That seems to be more important to her than anything else.

CHAPTER 3

A Feeling She Never Felt Before

It's October 16, 1995. Amanda has gotten pretty good at managing the store. Amanda is starting up the ice cream machine when Ryan and Mack came walking into the store. She talks to them and jokes with them as she always had done.

When they get to the register, Mack says to Amanda, "Ryan's leaving us. They're putting him at different job site."

Then Ryan looks right into Amanda's eyes and says, "They're divorcing us."

It is almost like he is trying to say something.

Right then, Amanda is trying to keep the tears from coming from her eyes. It isn't until that very moment that Amanda realized she is in love with Ryan. Amanda thinks, *How can this be?* She has loved before but somehow she knows it is different this time. Ryan and Mack leave the store and Amanda goes straight down the stairs to the basement where the storage area is; nobody ever came down there and she just starts crying. When she gets down to the basement and while crying, for the first time in twenty-three years, Amanda falls to the floor and prays to God. "Father, please let him come back to see me. I love him."

She cries and feels things she never felt before about anyone. You see, for the first time in Amanda's life, she finds out what real love feels like. It's not so much what you say or do. It's this feeling you get inside when the other person is around. Your stomach turns into knots and you're nervous. When they leave, you're sad and wish they never had to go away. I know what you're thinking, well something had to happen between them to make her feel this way. Well, I can assure you she never even kissed him, not even once.

When Amanda gets off work that day, she goes home and just keeps to herself. She doesn't want Tom to know she is crying. So she stays in another room of the house. Tom walks into the room however and finds her crying.

He asks her, "What is wrong, Amanda?"

She just looks at him and says, "I had a bad day at work."

Amanda doesn't think it is a good time to tell him how she feels.

The next day at work, Amanda is really sad when, all of a sudden, Ryan and Mack walk in. Amanda is really surprised because yesterday was supposed to be his last day here.

Amanda looks at Ryan and says, "I thought you weren't going to be here anymore."

Ryan, being sarcastic, says, "Well I thought I would stop by here on my way to my new job. Mack's dropping me off."

Ryan is acting strangely, almost like something is bothering him. I don't exactly know why but Amanda could feel he is upset over something. Amanda is not sure what but she could feel what he is feeling. He is looking around and he makes some comment to Amanda.

"This place looks filthy."

That really hurt Amanda's feelings because for weeks since she took over the store, she has been cleaning up the basement. When she gets done cleaning the basement, she is going to start on the upstairs next and clean it up. Amanda didn't understand why Ryan is being so mean to her.

Amanda looks over at the magazine rack and she says to him, "Will you come back and see me sometime?"

Ryan answers like it really didn't matter to him. "If I can, I will. Mack will still be around to see you."

Then they both walk out of the store and leave. Amanda thinks that maybe she should leave the store and not work there anymore.

She thinks if Ryan isn't going to come in anymore there is no point of her staying there because it would hurt too much. She thinks about what he said to her and he was right when he said, "You will miss me if I was gone." Amanda is really puzzled whether or not it is him that her mother had been telling her about and if it is him, then why is he leaving? Amanda knows she never loved anyone like this before.

Amanda later on in the day called Mary.

"Mom, can I come to see you?"

Mary says, "Sure, we can sit and talk in your car again like we did before."

When Amanda gets there, Mary is waiting for her. Amanda didn't want Mary to know that she fell in love with someone. Amanda knows deep down inside her heart that it is the man that her mother had described to her. Is it possible that it is a coincidence that Ryan looks like the man her mother had said?

Mary gets into Amanda's car and says, "How are you?"

Amanda replies, "I could be better. I wanted to see you because I'm curious about this man you told me about."

Mary's like, "Do you believe me now?"

"No, I'm not saying that. I just want you to tell me more about him. Let's just say, I'm curious."

Mary wonders why all of a sudden the interest when before Amanda would not even listen to her. Mary says, "What would you like to know about him?"

Amanda answers and says, "I just want to know some of the things you know."

Amanda knows the only way she would know if her mother is telling her the truth is to know things about him that were true, or that she could find out whether or not they were true.

Mary looks at Amanda and says, "Here is what I know. He had a good childhood. He got hurt once when he was younger on his bicycle and I think he even still has a scar from it. He had a swing in his backyard. He liked to comb his hair a lot when he was younger. He has two brothers and one of them has different hair color than his own. One of them had something to do with music, possibly a band. Either Ryan or one of his brothers listens to the Beatles a lot.

He loved someone once very deeply but he's never loved anyone in that way again until now."

Amanda says, "What do you mean until now?"

Mary responds and says, "Someday you will find out but that is years from now."

Amanda says to her, "Well, what else do you know?"

Mary continues telling her info about him. "His mother has grey hair but dyes it sometimes. His father is going bald on top. He has a blue car or he is going to buy one soon. One thing I do know for sure is that he can feel you and you can feel him but neither one of you knows why. I am sorry but that is all I am allowed to tell you for now."

Amanda asks her, "Mom, how will I know if it is him?"

"Soon he will hold you close to him. That will give you a clue as to who it is," Mary explains to her.

"You are kidding right. That doesn't make any sense." Amanda doesn't understand what she is trying to tell her.

Mary looks at Amanda and says, "Soon you will understand."

Amanda never tells Mary she is in love with Ryan. Could it be him that her mother's been telling her about? Could it be possible that her mother's telling the truth? Even though at this time Amanda still doesn't believe her mother completely, she feels she needed to find out the truth.

Then on December 22, 1995, it's just a few days before Christmas again. The store Amanda works at is closing today and will not be open again until January 2, 1996. Since the day Amanda started working there, they would close two weeks of the holiday break. Amanda has a lot to do to get everything prepared for not being there. Shutting the pop coolers down, taking things that would expire to another store to be sold while she is gone, cleaning things up, emptying the ice machine, and doing other things to prepare for the store not being open.

At one point during the day, she is downstairs working. She hears someone yell for her. She walks upstairs to see who it was. After she gets up the stairs, Mack and Ryan are standing there. The three of them stand there talking for a while. When they are getting ready to leave, Amanda decides she wants to mess with Mack before he leaves because he didn't talk to her as much as Ryan did. He is more distant than Ryan is.

"So, Mack, where's my Christmas hug?"

"I suppose I can do that," Mack says, as he reaches over and puts his arm around her for a second. He just kind of pats her on the back and says, "There you are, Merry Christmas."

Amanda didn't ask Ryan for a hug because she thinks he would just say no. Then Mack speaks up and says, "What about Ryan?"

Amanda looks at him and says, "What about Ryan?"

Mack smiles and says, "He probably wants one too."

He is standing there listening to what she and Mack are saying anyway. So Amanda walks close to where he is standing.

Ryan, with his beautiful blue eyes, says to her, "Yeah, I'll take a hug."

So they both put their arms around each other. They both stand there like neither one of them wants to let go. Ryan is taller than Amanda and so she put her head on his shoulder. After standing there for a minute and a half, they both back away from each other. Amanda never had anyone hold her that way. He is sturdy and strong and he held her tightly. She could even hear his heart beating.

After the hug, Amanda looks at him and says, "Merry Christmas, Ryan."

Ryan looks back at her and says, "Merry Christmas to you."

Mack speaks up and says, "We have to go back to work now. Have a good Christmas, Amanda."

Then they both walk out the door.

Amanda still hasn't told Ryan that she is in love with him. She is afraid that if she does he will never come back again. While Amanda is standing there thinking about how tight he held her, she realizes what her mother had said, "Soon he will hold you close to him. That will give you a clue as to who it is." Then a tear rolls down from Amanda's cheek. She realizes that maybe it is him. The only question she had is how she is ever going to be sure.

Amanda is finally able to leave work and go home. She is happy that she wouldn't have to work for two weeks. She knows however that she would miss Ryan very much.

It's Christmas Eve. Amanda is downstairs alone wrapping presents for tomorrow. Tom and the children are already asleep. She gets to play Santa Claus. When she is done putting the ribbons and bows on everything, she sits down in front of the Christmas tree with the lights all lit up. It is so beautiful.

She decides it is time she says a prayer. "Lord, I don't understand what's going on but I know I love Ryan. Where that love came from only you know. Has my mother been telling the truth? Was it you that put this love in my heart? I hope someday I'll understand the meaning of all this. I promise I'll try and listen better and understand. Amen." Amanda gets up from in front of the tree and goes to sleep.

It's Christmas Day 1995. Just as always, Amanda's parents come over. They eat dinner together and sit around talking. Amanda and her mom walk into the kitchen to put the plates up when Mary asks Amanda, "Is there anything you want to tell me?" It is almost like she knows what is going on inside of Amanda even without Amanda saying anything.

"No, Mom! I'm fine."

Amanda knows that's not how she really felt. Mary drops it after Amanda answers her. She thinks it is best not to press the issue.

After Amanda's parents leave and go home, Tom and the children go to bed. Amanda stays awake for a little while by herself. When something is bothering her, she just likes to be alone without anyone else around her, so Amanda decides to sit on the floor in front of the Christmas tree. Amanda never got anything for Christmas that day; Tom never usually bought her anything for Christmas anyways or for any other holiday for that matter. After a while, she got used to it being that way so she didn't expect anything from anyone after that.

Amanda however always spent her money on Tom, her children, and her parents. To her, the greatest Christmas gift she received that year is one that couldn't be bought. That is just getting to hold

Ryan close to her even though it was only for a moment. The main question Amanda has is would she have the nerve to tell him someday that she is in love with him or if she does, would he believe her? I guess only time can answer that question.

CHAPTER 4

Missing Him

Today is January 2, 1996, the first day of the opening of Amanda's store again. She wonders if Ryan missed her as much as she missed him. Amanda is hoping that Ryan would come in today on her first day back, but he never did. You see every day for a year and a half Ryan came in just about the same time every morning. He would usually buy coffee, donuts, and sometimes a newspaper if he felt like it. There were times he never bought anything at all. Amanda thinks that maybe on those days he came in and didn't purchase anything that he was just there to see her.

When Ryan had moved areas in October of 1995, she didn't get to see him as much. It made Amanda very sad. She felt lost, confused, and thought maybe she should leave. The only reason she stayed there as long as she has isn't for the money but just to be where he is. So the next day she starts looking for another job. She receives one offer from another convenience store. They give her two weeks to decide whether or not she wants to take it.

On January 17, almost before the two weeks are up, Mack and Ryan came in. It is so busy in the store that Amanda couldn't get away from the register and talk to Ryan. She wants to tell him she is leaving. The whole time Ryan is there, he is standing and talking to other guys he knows so it was hard for Amanda to get his attention.

Finally, when he is getting ready to walk out the door, Amanda stops him and says, "I'm leaving."

Ryan, with a puzzled look on his face, says, "When?"

Amanda speaks up and says, "Soon."

Ryan looks at her and says, "Don't worry. I'll be back."

Amanda didn't have a chance to tell him she only has until tomorrow to give her answer because he already walked out the door. When she gets home that night, she keeps thinking about what it is she wants to do. He moved areas and yet he still came over there to see her when he doesn't have to come to see her at all. Amanda knows if she leaves she would never have the chance to tell him she loves him. What is she going to do?

The next day, she waits before calling the other store and giving them her answer. She wants to see if he was going to come in so she could tell him how she felt, but again he never came in. She decides there is only one thing left for her to do and that is not to take the job. She doesn't feel she could leave him without telling him that she loves him. So she decides to stay and hopes that he would come back.

It's January 30, 1996. A few days have passed by and he finally comes back in to see her. She is standing on the back line making coffee for everybody when she looks over at him and says, "I've decided to stay."

Ryan looks at her and says, "Yeah."

Amanda decides to ask him a question and see what he says.

"You didn't want me to leave did you?"

Ryan simply says, "No!"

Then he buys what he wants and leaves again. Every time he walks out the store Amanda wonders if he would be back. She always hopes he would but there are no guarantees. Amanda wishes he would see how she feels without her having to tell him, but sometimes people are blind to what's right in front of them.

A long time passed and he still hasn't been back to see her. Maybe Amanda is just fooling herself thinking that she would ever be able to tell him how she feels.

Then on March 7, surprisingly enough, he came to see her. Now Amanda wrote a letter to him not only telling him how she feels but also what her mother told her. She didn't tell him exactly everything, just about what she said about the man she was to meet.

She is very surprised to see him. She had kept the letter for a long time, hoping she would have the nerve to give it to him. So here is her chance to do so. The only question she had is whether or not he would believe her. I guess it would be hard for anybody to believe Amanda.

So when Ryan walks over to the register, she hands him the letter. She also wonders what he would think of her now, but she knows she had to try. You see, she knows in her heart that she loves him more than she's ever loved anyone and she had to tell him. Even if it meant he doesn't believe her.

The next day, she expects him to come back in and say something to her, but he never did. She is very upset. Then finally on March 11, he came in. She thinks maybe he had to think about what she said. She is a little angry with him so instead of asking him what he thinks about the letter, she is mean to him instead.

A few days later on March 14, Ryan and Mack came into the store again. Amanda walks over by the ATM machine where he is standing and says to him, "I'm sorry if I was mean to you the other day."

Ryan looks at her and says, "That's okay, you weren't really."

Amanda looks into his eyes, afraid of what he must be thinking of her, and says, "Do you forgive me?"

Ryan just simply says, "Yeah."

When they are done purchasing what they want, they leave. Now Ryan didn't say anything about the letter at all. So Amanda decides she better not press the issue. Trying to make him believe is going to be harder than her mother trying to convince her it is true. Amanda feels really stupid now because she thinks maybe it is wrong for her to tell him what she did.

It's March 27, 1996. Mary calls to see how Amanda is doing.

"Hi, Amanda, how are you doing today? I haven't seen you for a while."

"No, Mom, I'm not okay. Can I come down there and talk to you?"

Amanda is really upset and didn't know what to think or do now. Amanda thinks it is time to tell her mother she thinks she knows who it is that she's been telling her about. So Amanda drives down to her house and Mary gets into her car.

"Mom, I have some things to tell you."

Amanda starts explaining everything to her mother. Her mother just sits there and listens.

"I think I know who the man is you have been telling me about. I have known him for a while now and I have fallen in love with him. What I don't understand is why did he have to move areas right when I was getting close to him?"

When she is finished, her mother says, "I already knew that you have fallen in love with this man. I also know if he would not have left, then you would not have realized you loved him. Do you believe what I told you yet?"

"You mean about what happened to you when you died, I don't know what to believe anymore. If this is coming from some higher power, then tell me more."

"Let me tell you what you didn't tell me." Mary goes on to tell Amanda things that Amanda didn't tell her about such as things that Ryan and she talked about and other things that have happened between them. There were things that Mary told Amanda that there is no way she could have known. The moment she truly believed her during this conversation is when Mary said the one thing that she had never told anyone ever. Mary tells her she knows that her uncle had raped her. When this happened to Amanda, her mom was ill and the only way she could have known it is if God himself had shown it to her. Amanda just sits there in shock about what she is hearing.

When Mary is done, Amanda says to her, "How did you know all that?"

Mary simply says, "The Lord showed me."

Before Mary gets out of the car, Mary looks at her and says, "You won't see him for a while in your store, but he will be back. Just keep an eye out on your way home every day and by the way, Amanda, he is your soul mate."

Amanda has no idea what she is talking about and then she drives home.

Mary is right. Forty-five days passed and Ryan never came into the store. Amanda is so hurt; she thinks it is because of what she told him that he is never coming back. During that time, Amanda saw him four times on her way home. Once, they pull up next to each other and just said hi.

Amanda just could not understand why he never came in to see her. During this time, she cries a lot and is very sad. Finally, one day, she is sitting and crying and Tom sees her. He decides to ask her what is wrong.

"Amanda, why are you crying? What is wrong with you lately? You haven't been acting like yourself for quite a while."

Amanda looks at him, almost afraid to tell him, "I'm sorry if this hurts you but I'm in love with Ryan."

Tom's sitting there, stunned, says to Amanda, "Who is Ryan and why didn't you tell me before now?"

"I didn't know how to tell you. I was afraid of hurting you," Amanda says to him in this quiet voice.

Amanda goes on to tell Tom what her mother told her and that she cared about him but because of the way he's treated her she could never love him like she loved Ryan. Amanda tried over the last ten years to love Tom, but he never understood how Amanda felt. He doesn't understand that to her love is something that came from inside of you. That's probably why up until now she never truly loved anyone.

Every time Amanda tries to get close to anyone, they always hurt her. Ryan might have said things sometimes or did things that bothered Amanda and made her cry, but he never intentionally tried to hurt her.

Tom seems to be angry with Amanda and bitter toward her, but what he didn't realize is what he's never done, and that was for him to stop holding on to hate within himself and being mean to Amanda. The more he acts mean toward her, the more Amanda pulls away from him. So Tom and Amanda decide to stay together for the children. Amanda knows that Tom cares about her but he could never seem to stop being bitter long enough to see how he's treated her.

Amanda's only wish for Tom is that maybe someday he'll open his eyes and let go of his hate and realize she never meant to hurt him, but she couldn't stop how she feels even if she wanted to. He never really treats her like he should. With any luck at all, someday, he'll understand and forgive her. Hopefully, he'll realize what kind of person Amanda is and she could truly never hurt anyone on purpose. This is the last time she ever talks to Tom about Ryan and she's never brought it up since. Amanda knows no matter what Tom says or does, it is not going to change the way she feels toward Ryan.

CHAPTER 5

Eye-Opening Discoveries

It's May 15, 1996. Amanda's at work and she's very tired. She's just doing what needs to be done when all of a sudden Ryan walks in. Amanda practically swallows her heart. She just couldn't believe it.

Ryan gets a cup of coffee and walks over to the register. Then he says to her, "I missed my mocha."

Mocha is a cappuccino drink he has every time he ever comes in to see her. When he says what he says, he has this strange look in his eyes like he is trying to say something. Amanda gave him the nickname "the riddler," because he would say things to her but he would never just come out and say what he meant. He would talk in rhythms and riddles. He didn't realize but Amanda always knows what he means. After Ryan says he missed his mocha, Amanda just looked at him and didn't say anything.

Ryan speaks up and says, "So, how are you?"

"I'm okay. I have just been working a lot of hours," Amanda says back to him.

"I know you have. I haven't come to see you because I didn't have transportation over here."

Amanda feels he is just making excuses that maybe he didn't want to come to see her, but then again she could have been wrong. After Ryan is done buying what he wanted, he leaves.

The next day, Amanda goes to see her mother after work.

"Mom, will you please tell me more about him?"

Her mom says, "Sure, I can tell you more. What do you want to know?"

"What kind of things does Ryan like or anything else about him I should know?"

"Well, he likes to play games, he drinks once in a while, and he plays golf. He also went to the same high school you did."

"What else does he like?" Amanda is really curious now about everything her mother knew.

Mary looks at Amanda and says, "Do you want to know it all now?"

Very curious, Amanda says to Mary, "Yes, tell me everything you can."

"Okay, if that's what you want. He likes movies, he likes sports. He's a very kind and gentle person. When he gets mad though he likes to be left alone until he's not mad anymore. He gets really quiet when something's bothering him. He has a son and a daughter."

Right then Amanda interrupts her and says, "He has a son that I know of but he does not have a daughter. In the two years, I have known him he has never said anything about a daughter, neither has anyone else."

Mary says, "It's true, he has a daughter. She may not be his real daughter but to him she is. He loves her just as much even though she doesn't want to do what he tells her to do. Sometimes she talks back to him and gives him a hard time. Every once in a while she says things to hurt his feelings but so does his wife. Now do you want to hear more about him?"

"Sure, tell me more, but I still can't believe he has a daughter." Amanda is really surprised about that.

"He's going to have a family member die in a few years. I see him helping carry the gasket and I also see him standing in front of it wearing a suit and the casket I think is grey. Here, real soon, he is going to build a house. It will have bricks in it. There will be flowers in the yard. He will move to a town where you went to church as a child. He's having financial problems but he's trying to fix them. His wife likes to spend too much money sometimes and that upsets him. He doesn't really believe you love him like you say you do but someday he will realize you do. He tries to keep up with everybody else; having nice things and new things he likes, but he has forgotten what's really important to him. He also will have other responsibilities more than he does now. He may one day become a supervisor. During the summer, he works really long hours and he works hard. You will talk to him on the phone soon. The Lord says that's all I can tell you for now. Within the next two years, you will understand. Go home and read your Bible and some things will become clear."

So Amanda leaves and goes home. That must have been the longest conversation they ever had between them.

Amanda starts reading her Bible that day for the first time in her life. While she is reading it, she finds a scripture that is very interesting to her. It is in *Deuteronomy* chapter 18:

> The Lord said to me: "What they say is good. I will raise up for them a prophet like you from among their brothers; I will put my words in his mouth, and he will tell them everything I command him. If anyone does not listen to my words that the prophet speaks in my name, I myself will call him to account. But a prophet who presumes to speak in my name anything I have not commanded him to say, or a prophet who speaks in the name of other gods, must be put to death. You may say to yourselves, how can we know when a message has not been spoken by the Lord? If what the prophet proclaims does not take place or come true, that message the Lord has not spoken. (Deuteronomy 18:17–22)

Amanda wonders if her mom could be a prophet and if that is true, why she was chosen to give the messages to Amanda. What is it about Amanda that is different that the Lord would choose her to know these things? And what is it that the Lord wants Amanda to do and why? Amanda knew she didn't believe in psychics, she thinks they are not real, but what is happening to her is all coming true. Could it possibly be that what her mother says is true and that it isn't her mother telling her these things but God? I guess only time can tell her the truth, but first, she has to believe in what she doesn't understand.

On May 20, 1996, Amanda is downstairs working when she hears someone yell at her. She isn't exactly sure who it was so she walks to the bottom of the stairs and at the top of the stairs that Ryan was standing there.

"Hi, Ryan, what are you doing here?"

"I was on my way somewhere and I thought I would stop and say hi. I only have a few minutes," Ryan says to her.

Amanda looks at him and says, "Well, come down here for a second."

So Ryan walks downstairs to see her. Amanda is standing by the fax machine and she tells him to wait a minute. The room is so quiet and there is no one else around. When she is done faxing her donut order, she walks over to where he is standing. She is so close to him that she put her hands on his chest and looks straight into his eyes. Now Amanda thinks about kissing him but instead she just says, "I just wanted a hug." So she just gives him a hug and steps back away from him.

He acts really scared and says, "I've got to go."

Ryan starts walking away.

Amanda says, "Have a good day."

Then up the stairs he goes, as fast as he could. What she didn't understand is what scared him. Was it her feelings for him that scared him? Amanda wanted to kiss him but she knew that she wasn't supposed to. It had to be up to him to decide whether he loved her or not. Amanda knows that if he is to love her, it has to come from inside his heart as it did hers and not from anything else. The rest of the day, Amanda just keeps thinking about what happened.

On June 11, 1996, Amanda's really busy and the phone is ringing off the wall. Amanda walks over to the phone to pick it up again. She says the name of the store and then hears a man's voice.

The man says, "Do you have any eggs today?" He says it in a really nice voice.

Amanda says, "Yes, I have some left."

"Thank you," the man on the phone replies.

Amanda says, "You're welcome."

Then he hangs up and so does she.

After she hung up the phone, she has this strange feeling that she knows that voice. For some reason, she feels it was Ryan. Then about an hour and a half later, Mack and Ryan came in. She is busy and doesn't pay much attention to him. When he gets over to the register, he doesn't say a word but then Amanda noticed that there was a carton of eggs in his hand. When she looks into his face and eyes, he smiles, and right then she knew it was him that she talked to on the phone.

He says to her, "I need eggs to cook with."

Amanda says, "Yeah, I see this."

She rang the eggs up and then Mack and Ryan leave. Mary again is telling her the truth. She did speak to him on the phone.

It's August 7, 1996. Amanda unlocks the doors to the store so customers could come in. Now usually first thing in the morning it's really quiet and slow between six and seven. It's about 6:30 a.m., and Ryan walks into the store. He is all alone and he seems to be in a good mood.

He says to Amanda, "Hi, Amanda."

Amanda says, "Hello. What are you doing in here so early today? Are you doing something special today?"

"Well, I'm going to play golf this afternoon," Ryan explains.

"Oh yeah, have you ever tried to play Frisbee golf?" Amanda asks him.

"I haven't played Frisbee since high school," Ryan tells her.

"Oh yeah, what high school did you go to?" Amanda asks him.

"I went to Central," he says back to her.

Amanda just about falls over because those are two of the things that her mother told her.

Amanda looks at him and says, "So you like to golf do you?"

Ryan says, "Yeah. Listen do me a favor and don't send my donuts anymore. I appreciate it but I prefer you didn't."

Now, in a way, that hurt Amanda's feelings because every day he didn't come in, she would send donuts and coffee with Mack to give to him. She doesn't want anything from him. She is just trying to be nice.

Ryan finally says to Amanda, "Well, I'll see you later."

Then Ryan walks out of the store.

Later on that morning Mack, Bill, Ralph, and Burt, who is the new guy, came into the store. They start talking about the donuts she was sending Ryan and is teasing her about it. Then she understood that his friends must be teasing him about her and that's why he didn't want her to do it anymore. What his friends didn't understand is that what is going on between Amanda and Ryan is something higher than both of them. Amanda loves him, yes, but they are just friends even though Amanda wishes he loves her too. So when they would say things sometimes about Ryan, it would hurt her more than they realized.

She also finds out from Mack today that Ryan is building a house just like her mother had said. The more she gets to know Ryan, the more things she finds are true. Everything that she is learning about him is just like her mother told her. Amanda, still being skeptical, wonders how her mother could have known all that she did.

It's October 10, 1996, Ryan and Mack came into the store together and Amanda had kept a letter to give him. In the letter, she tells him about her mother again and talked about what he has meant to her all this time. At the end of the letter, she says, "What I need to know from you is do you care? If I don't hear from you this time, I'll know you never cared for me at all."

Now she makes sure he receives the letter before he leaves the store. She wonders if he would believe her now. The next day, first thing, just like a knight in shining armor, he came walking into the store. Amanda is so happy because to her that said he cared a little, otherwise, he wouldn't have bothered to ever come to see her again. Amanda thinks that he's never had reason to come back and see her, but he always has. Now he didn't say anything about the letter so later on that morning she calls him. She feels she had to know the truth. She knows the reason he didn't say anything about the letter is that there are so many people around.

So she picks up the phone and says, "Hi, Ryan. We really couldn't talk earlier. I need to know, do you care?"

Ryan says, "Not the way you want me to."

Amanda knew what he meant; maybe he didn't love her as much as she loved him, but in a way, he did care about her. So then she says to him, "Have I been a bother to you all this time?"

Ryan answers, "Not especially."

Amanda simply says, "Have a good weekend."

Then she just hangs up the phone. She is a little hurt by their conversation, but Amanda knows that even if she wants to she can't stop loving him. Though she tried, it was like something was pulling her toward him time and time again. Soon she would understand why.

A lot of time has passed and now it's December 20, 1996. Amanda is preparing to close the store for Christmas again. She hasn't seen Ryan yet to tell him Merry Christmas.

Mack walks in and says, "Hi, Amanda."

Amanda says, "Where's Ryan?"

Mack answers her and says, "He's out in the truck. He's not coming in today."

She says to Mack, "Doesn't he know the store closes today and he won't see me for two weeks?"

Mack says, "I don't think he realized it. Do you want me to go and get him?"

Amanda is really upset and says, "If he would rather stay out there instead of coming inside and saying Merry Christmas, let him."

Mack says, "Okay, well, Amanda you have a good Christmas."

Mack buys what he wants and leaves. Amanda is so hurt and upset. She thinks this is going to be the worst Christmas she will ever have since she became an adult. The reason is, the only person that she cares about or wants to say Merry Christmas to is acting like it doesn't even matter to him. Amanda knows she won't be back in her store for two weeks. Amanda thinks maybe he is upset with her for calling him, just maybe she should not have done so. What neither one of them understands is that a choice that Amanda is going to make in the next year coming up will change their lives forever, especially Amanda's.

CHAPTER 6

Don't Want to Leave

It's the beginning of another new year. Tom has been pressuring Amanda for a long time for her to leave her store since he found out the way she feels about Ryan. He has been even more cruel to her than he was before, accusing her of things she wasn't doing and just making her miserable.

So finally Amanda tells him she will leave her store but not until June 27, when she had her vacation. Now Amanda knows inside her heart she could never leave Ryan, even though she said she would. To her, nothing could separate her from him, but she is wrong.

It's January 8, 1997. Amanda's standing at the register talking to a few of the other guys that come into the store. Amanda is standing there laughing and kidding with them when Ryan and Mack walk in.

Ryan says, "Hey, you're back."

Amanda just ignores him. The two weeks her store was closed she had been working at another store right down the street, instead of taking a vacation like she did last year. Ryan never came to see her or calls so she is upset and mad at him. He knows where she is and even drove by a couple of times but never once stopped. She wonders if she ever did leave whether she would see him again or whether or not he would even care if she wasn't there at all.

When Ryan and Mack get to the register, Amanda says, "Hi, Mack."

Mack says, "Hey, Amanda. How are you?"

Ryan stands there and acts like he wants Amanda to say hi to him too. So finally she says, "Hi, Ryan."

Ryan looks at her and says, "So how was the other store?"

Amanda says, "It was okay. I got to manage someone else's employees but no one ever came to see me."

She is making a hint to Ryan that he had hurt her feelings. Ryan just looks at her and says nothing.

Then Mack says, "Well, you ready to go, Ryan?"

Ryan replies, "Yes."

Then they both leave the store.

It's January 17, 1997. Today just about everyone has come into the store. It's 10:00 a.m., Ralph and Burt just came walking in.

Burt says, "Hi, Amanda."

So she stands there and starts talking to Ralph and Burt.

Burt says, "So, Amanda, has Ryan been in today to see you?"

Amanda says, "No, not yet."

Burt then asks her," You really like him don't you?"

Amanda says, "Yeah but he makes me nervous."

Burt says, "Why does he make you nervous?"

Right when Amanda was going to say why Ryan makes her nervous, Ryan and Mack walk in.

Ryan says, "What's going on in here?"

So Burt walks over to Ryan and says, "Watch out, man, she's going to get nervous now that you're here."

Ryan just gets this strange look on his face. He didn't understand what Burt was talking about.

Then Burt thought he would tease Ryan and Ralph.

Burt says to Amanda, "Hey, Amanda! Look at this, your two favorite men right here."

Now Amanda likes Ralph but just as a friend. She thinks he is a very nice friend to have. To her, all of them are good friends except Ryan. Nobody seems to understand how much she cares about Ryan. It is not some crush. His friends only know what they see, but they don't know there is something more to it. In a sense, they know she really likes him, but I don't think any of them understands that she is in love with him.

Finally, Ralph and Burt think it is time to leave. When Ralph is walking out the door, he says to Ryan, "She's all yours now."

When Amanda worked in the store, she usually had one other person that always worked with her. For the last six months, it is a guy named Curtis. He is young and full of energy all the time. Amanda thinks maybe she should tell Ryan and Mack it is Curtis's last day.

Amanda says to them, "Hey, guess what, Ryan, today is Curtis's last day."

Ryan says, "Oh yeah! Where are you going?"

Curtis says, "I'm going back home. I have finished school down here."

Ryan says, "I can see a tear coming from your eye because you're going to miss Amanda, aren't you?"

Curtis answers him and says, "No, it's not."

Ryan says, "Yes, it will."

Curtis decides he would tell him that Amanda is leaving too. So he says to Ryan, "Did you know Amanda's leaving too?

Ryan says, "No!"

Curtis says, "Yeah at the end of June."

Ryan says to Amanda, "You're leaving us, when?"

Amanda answers him, "June 27 will be my last day here."

Ryan says to her, "You'll never leave here."

Ryan might have wanted to believe that it is true and if Amanda has her choice, she would not ever leave him, but unfortunately, she doesn't have her choice because Tom isn't going to let her stay. After they all stood there talking for a few more minutes, Ryan and Mack decide it is time to leave.

After they left, Curtis says to Amanda, "You realize that conversation me and Ryan had about crying and missing you was him more or less referring to himself."

Amanda says to Curtis, "You think he was talking about himself?"

Curtis says, "Yes. I think he's trying to say he would miss you."

Amanda says, "I doubt it. He doesn't care about me. I even asked him once and all he could say is not the way you want me to."

A part of Amanda always wished he cares a little more than he would admit but she knows he would never say it not until the day he is ready to.

It's February 5, 1997, Amanda's birthday. Just like Christmas, she only wants one thing for her birthday and that is just to be able to see Ryan. At least this time, she gets what she wished for. It is very early in the morning when Mack and Ryan came into the store.

Amanda says to them, "Hey, you guys are early."

Ryan says, "We want to beat the morning rush. By the way, Amanda, happy birthday."

Amanda says, "Thank you."

Ryan then says, "Where is Diane at?"

Amanda says, "She must have overslept."

Ryan says, "You're too nice."

Amanda says, "You wouldn't want me to be mean would you?"

Ryan just says to her, "No."

Now Diane is the girl she is working with since Curtis left. Amanda had worked with Diane for a year before Curtis. Then Diane quit and now she came back to work again. Amanda is standing there talking to them and decides to be silly. She grabs an empty pop bottle from beside the register and spun it on the counter. Amanda says to them, "Whose turn is it?" Mack and Ryan just start laughing.

Ryan says, "I was more partial to truth or dare myself."

Amanda says, "You were, were you."

Ryan says to Amanda, "Which one did you pick?"

Amanda says, "Truth."

Ryan says, "Yeah, lies always catch up with you."

After their conversation, Ryan and Mack leave the store.

The only things that Amanda would never know whether or not they were true are the things about his childhood. She could never bring herself to ask him about them. She didn't even know anything about his family. Did he have any siblings? Mary told Amanda once that he had a hard time believing that she loves him. Amanda has told Ryan a lot about the things her mother had told her, but there are other things she never told him. Amanda knows if she truly didn't believe it herself, then how would she be able to ever convince him to believe her?

February 20, 1997, Amanda is so happy tomorrow is Friday. She is tired and could use a day off. When Mack walks in without Ryan, Amanda says, "Where's Ryan?"

Mack says, "He's at home, sick."

Amanda says, "So tell me did you give him his cold?"

Mack says, "It wasn't me it was probably his kids."

Amanda says, "Kids? I thought he only had a son."

Mack says, "No, he has a stepdaughter too."

Amanda, with a surprised look on her face, says, "How old is she?"

Mack says, "She's seventeen."

Amanda says, "I just can't believe he has a daughter."

Mack says, "I guess there are a lot of things you don't know about Ryan."

Amanda says, "I guess you're right."

Mack says, "Well, Amanda, hope you have a good day. I will talk to you later."

Then Mack walks out of the store.

Amanda has a hard time believing that her mother is right again. She still has a hard time understanding how her mother could know so much about this man. Amanda's starting to think maybe she has been telling her the truth. Maybe there is a higher being such as God who is doing all this. Even though she is still a little skeptical, she can't help but wonder if it is all true. Could it be that this is a message from heaven and why did God choose her?

It is March 10, 1997. It's a beautiful day outside. Amanda just wishes she is outside instead of in the store. It's break time again when most of the employees around come into the store. Just like any other day, Amanda hopes that Mack and Ryan would come in and see her. When they walk in, it is about 10:00 a.m.

Mack says, "Good morning, Amanda."

Ryan just says, "Hi!"

Amanda says to Ryan, "Are you okay?"

Ryan says, "I'm still sick."

Amanda says, "I'm sorry. I hope you feel better soon because I care about you."

Ryan says, "You seem to be the only one who does."

Mack speaks up and says, "You should be a nurse."

Amanda says, "No, I've always wanted to be a teacher."

Ryan says, "I'm going to have surgery on my nose."

Amanda says, "Is it dangerous?"

Ryan says, "There are some risks."

Amanda then says, "Will you do me a favor?"

Ryan says, "What?"

Amanda says, "Will you promise to let me know you're okay?"

Ryan says, "Well if you see me again I guess you will know I'm not dead."

Amanda says, "Don't say that."

Ryan says, "Why?"

Amanda says, "If you die, you would be taking a part of me with you."

When she says it, she wonders what made her say that just then. Is it possible that he is her soul mate? Ryan stands there and doesn't say anything. Then Mack and Ryan decide it is time to leave. So they both walk out the door.

That night, Amanda goes home and says a prayer. "Lord! Please let him pull through his surgery okay. Amen!" Then Amanda is tired and goes to sleep.

The next few months go very quickly and Amanda is running out of time. She thinks she had better prepare for her leaving the store. The main thing she cares about is trying to tell Ryan again how much he meant to her. She thinks if he hadn't realized it by now, then he never will.

Amanda decides it is time to write the longest letter of her life to Ryan. She has only one more chance to make him see how much she really did love him even if he didn't believe her. More than anything in this world, she wishes he would ask her to stay. If only he believed her, then he could see she could have never done anything to hurt him. She loves him more than she ever thought she would love any-one, even more importantly, she loves him enough to die for him. If there is a choice between her life and his, she would choose for him to live and she would give her life to save his.

CHAPTER 7

The Last Goodbye

Over the next few months, Diane quit again. Amanda starts working with a guy named Dwayne. Dwayne is a really nice guy. He has a girl-friend named Allison. They would sometimes stand around and joke about things. Dwayne never really understood what exactly is going on between Ryan and Amanda but he knows how much Amanda cares for Ryan.

Ryan is still coming to see Amanda and sometimes it seems like they are getting closer than they were before. It isn't so much what is said between them, but it is the little things they shared that made the difference.

Today is June 26, 1997. Amanda has been preparing to leave all week. She is so upset she didn't know how she could. She loves Ryan so much she knows it is going to tear her apart. It's really early in the morning and Ryan just walks in.

Ryan says, "So this is it."

Amanda says, "Yeah, I guess so."

Ryan says, "I will see you again sometime."

Amanda says, "This is for you."

She hands Ryan an envelope. Inside, there's a picture they took together last year and a letter telling him goodbye.

Over the next few days, Amanda is so sad. She even stops eat-ing. She feels life isn't worth living anymore. For the first time in

Amanda's life, she truly loves someone and to her, it feels like her life is over. Later on in the next few weeks, Amanda finds out that the new manager that they hired has already quit.

Tom is really getting upset with Amanda because of the way she is acting. He says to her, "Are you going to be like this the rest of your life?"

Amanda says, "Yes."

Tom finally says, "Okay. You can go back to your store if it will stop you from crying and moping around here all day."

So then on July 15, she is allowed to go back to her store. She is so happy because she didn't want to leave to begin with. She gets to see Ryan again and she is very excited. She thinks that she would never leave him again and there is nothing on this earth that could separate them.

Her first day back, Mack came into the store.

He says, "Hey, what are you doing here?"

Amanda says, "The manager they had quit and so I came back."

She couldn't tell everybody the truth of why she came back. She knows that they wouldn't understand.

The next day, Mack brings Ryan in. Now I guess Mack kept it from Ryan that she is there. Ryan is getting his drink when he sees her and he says, "Hey! What are doing here?"

Amanda says, "The new manager they hired had quit."

Ryan says, "I knew you would never leave me."

Amanda says, "It seems like it. Every time I have a chance to leave here something stops me."

Ryan says, "Maybe it's fate keeping you here."

Amanda wonders when he says that if he is starting to believe her now. I guess only time could tell them that. Amanda is just so happy to be back where she feels she belongs. There is nothing else that matters to her. What Amanda didn't realize is that everything is about to change very quickly and she is going to have to make the hardest choice of her life.

It's Saturday, August 2, 1997. Amanda's cleaning the house and the phone rings. Amanda picks up the phone and says, "Hello."

On the other line is her mother. Mary says, "Hi, Amanda."

Amanda says, "Hi, Mom. What are you doing?"

Mary says, "Amanda, I really need to talk to you."

Amanda says, "What's wrong, Mom?"

She could tell by her mother's voice something seem wrong.

Mary says, "I can't tell you on the phone. Would you please come down here?"

Amanda says, "Sure, I'll be right there."

So Amanda finishes what she is doing and goes to see her mother. When she gets down there, her mother seemed bothered by something. Amanda walks in and says, "What's wrong mom?"

Mary says, "I have something to tell you that is probably going to hurt you."

Amanda says, "What are you talking about? You're not sick, are you? My father's okay, isn't he?"

Mary says, "Your father and I are fine. Someone else that you care about isn't going to be fine."

Amanda says, "Who is it?"

Mary says, "It's Ryan."

Amanda says, "Ryan. What's wrong with Ryan?"

Mary says, "I don't know how to tell you this but he's going to die in a car accident."

Amanda says, "No! It can't be true. Father, please don't let him die"

Mary says, "Do you love him?"

Amanda says, "You know I do."

Mary says, "Do you believe me now?"

Amanda says, "Yes. What do I have to do to save him from dying?"

Right when Amanda says that she realizes there is only one thing she could do. She gets down on her knees and she says, "Lord, please don't take his life. If you let him live I promise to leave him and you can take my life instead."

Then Amanda hears the same voice she had heard come from her mother that day in the car and it says, "It is as you say. You have up to the last day of the month."

Right then Amanda realizes it is not her mother but it is God that is talking through her mother. Just like the scripture says.

That very next Monday, Amanda tells the owners of the store that she is in fact resigning and that she isn't going to work there anymore. She tells them that August 31 will be her last day. It is hard for them to find a manager at first, but they finally do.

On August 26, 1997, just a few days before Amanda's last day, Mack and Ryan came into the store.

Amanda says to them, 'Well, guys, this is it."

Ryan says, "You'll be back again."

Amanda just answers and says, "Not this time."

After that, Ryan and Mack buy what they want and leave the store.

Amanda knows she could not tell him why she is leaving. He probably will not believe her anyway. It took her a very long time to believe it too and what she is told and why she is told the things that she is.

On Thursday, August 28, 1997, Amanda leaves for the bank. On her way, she sees Ryan walking up the street, she knows he is coming to say goodbye. When she gets back from the bank, she asks Dwayne if he had been there. Dwayne tells her yes. She never got to say goodbye to him. That hurt Amanda more than anything has ever hurt her in her life, even though deep down inside her she knows she is doing the right thing.

She does leave her store on August 29, 1997, never to work there again. Then on September 26, 1997, a month later, she feels that she needs to call him for the first time since she left. She wants to make sure he is still okay.

He is there and he picks up the phone and says, "Hello."

"Hi," Amanda says to him.

Ryan says, "Hi!"

Amanda says, "I called to see how everybody was doing."

Ryan says, "Everybody here is fine."

Amanda says, "There are some people that came to see me. I guess that means not everybody has forgotten about me."

Ryan says, "That could never happen."

Amanda says, "I miss my store."

Ryan says, "Your store?"

Amanda says, "I have always considered it my store."

Ryan then says, "It's here if you want to come back."

Amanda says, "I wish I could but I can't. I didn't bother you, did I?"

Ryan says, "I was just heading out the door to leave."

Amanda says, "Well, I better let you go. Take care of yourself."

Ryan says, "You too."

When she is at home that night, she sits by herself and prays. "Lord, please, watch over him always." As she is on her knees praying, the tears just flow from her eyes in the hope that she would see him again someday and know that he is okay.

CHAPTER 8

Her Last Wish

It's Saturday, December 10, 1997. Amanda has been away from Ryan for four months. Her heart is saddened and she wishes she could see him. Amanda decided to drive down to her mother's to talk to her for a moment.

When she gets into the house, she says, "Hi, Mom."

Mary says, "The answer to your question is yes, you will see him again."

Amanda's mom knows what she is going to ask her before she ever had the chance to say it.

Mary says, "You will see him while you're out shopping, but not a word will be spoken between you. I told you before he can feel you and you can feel him and neither one of you knows why, but now that you know the truth, you understand why you feel him when he is around, you also now understand why sometimes you dream about him and see his face before you all of a sudden and why you feel what he is feeling at times. He really is your soul mate." Then Mary says, "Go home and pray to God and he will answer you."

So Amanda did just that. A few days later on December 13, 1997, she feels very lonely and scared. She thinks there is nothing left for her. After Tom and the kids go to bed, Amanda bends down on her knees in front of the Christmas tree like she had so many other times before.

She says, "Lord! If you are listening, please show me he's okay. The only thing I want for Christmas this year is just to look at him and know I did the right thing."

The next day, December 14, 1997, Amanda goes to buy presents for Christmas. While she is shopping, she, in fact, sees him. She is walking through the mall getting ready to leave when she feels he is there, then out of the corner of her eye she sees him there. He is standing across from her at a little shop in the center of the mall. She doesn't say one word to him. It is almost like she is not able to talk.

She then looks at her children whom she had with her and says, "Okay, we can go now."

When she gets outside, she couldn't stop the tears from coming down. When the children ask her what is wrong, she says, "May he forgive me someday for leaving."

The children ask her what she is talking about but she doesn't answer them.

A few years had passed since that day and now it is June 29, 2000, it has been two and half years now since she last saw him and Amanda has been thinking about wanting to see Ryan or talk to him but there is a part of her that is scared whether she should. She just really wants to know if he is still alive. When she left her store back in 1997, she went to a different store for the same company. So before leaving for work, she picks up the phone and calls Mary to ask her if it is okay.

Amanda says to Mary when she picks up the phone, "Is he still living, Mom?"

Mary responds and simply says, "Yes."

Amanda says to her, "Would God be angry with me if I call to check on him?"

Mary answers her and says, "No."

So Amanda says to her, "Thank you."

Then Amanda hangs up the phone.

Once Amanda gets to work she goes ahead and makes a call to him. She is truly nervous about doing so. She isn't even sure what she would say to him after all this time. Amanda thinks, *What if he does not want to talk to her again and just hangs up the phone?*

The phone starts to ring and a voice comes on the line.

"Hello, this is Dennis."

Amanda says, "Hi, I would like to speak to Ryan please?"

Dennis answers and says, "He is not here right now. He is out on a job."

Amanda says to Dennis, "Well, this is an old friend of his and I have not spoken with him in years."

Dennis responds by saying, "Well, if you leave me your phone number, I will have him call you when he gets back if that is okay."

So Amanda hangs up the phone.

While she is working, Amanda thinks, *What if he does not call?* Maybe he won't want to talk to her again. It seems like forever had gone by even though it is only ten minutes when the phone had rung.

"Hi, thank you for calling The Pantry." (Now, of course, this is not the real name of where Amanda works at the time but I don't think it is a good idea to say the real name of the company she works for. We will just call it The Pantry.)

When she answers, there is dead silence on the line. I don't know if he is thinking about hanging up or whether he is just surprised about the call. He finally responds and says, "Hello."

Amanda responds to him, "I don't know if you know who this is but I am pretty sure you do."

Ryan just answers, "Yes, I know who this is."

"Well, it's been a very long time, almost three years since we had spoken and I just wanted to call and say hi," Amanda explains to him.

Ryan responds with a strange voice and says, "What is this like an anniversary call or something?"

Amanda answers and says, "Something like that."

Of course, Amanda could not tell him the truth about why she is calling. She just needs to know if he is still okay. Amanda continues by saying, "Did you wonder who it was that called you? I assume you didn't expect for it to be me."

Ryan answers and says, "Yeah, I did wonder who it was."

"So, tell me, are you a supervisor or foreman yet?" Mary told Amanda that someday he is going to take on an important role with his job. She says she thought it would be a supervisor position or something that is important.

Ryan answers her and says, "I don't want to be a babysitter. I would rather be babysat."

"Oh well, I am sorry if I had bothered you. I just wanted to say hi since it had been so long," Amanda continues by saying, "I assume you are well situated in your new home by now?"

Ryan says, "Yeah, for years now."

Amanda says back, "Well that is great. I hope you didn't mind me calling you."

Ryan then says to her, "You still working on the corner of Prospect and Springfield?"

Amanda answers him and says, "Yes, I am usually here from 7:00 a.m. to 1:00 p.m. every day."

Ryan then says, "Maybe I will stop in sometime and say hi."

Amanda responds back and says, "That would be nice. Well, I am sorry I bothered you at work. Take care of yourself."

He then says, "I will see you later," and hangs up.

After the conversation, she hopes he would not be angry with her for calling him. She did, however, start crying for a little while thinking back on what happened but knowing that he is still okay is really all she wants to know. Amanda at least knows she would have some peace for a little while getting to hear his voice again. More than anything in this world, she hopes to see him again but that is not up to her. When she gets home that day, she says a prayer to Father.

"Thank you, Father, for giving me a chance to talk to him again. Just knowing he is still okay and that you kept your promise to me is all I could have ever asked for. I promise you I will keep my promise to you that I made as a child when you saved me that day when I died. Amen." At this point, Amanda remembers what happened when she died that day and the message she was told to share.

Amanda sits there for a little bit when she realizes something— it is exactly six years to the date that she had met him on July 29,

1994, and it is almost three years since she left the store where he was at on August 29, 1997.

It is December 24, 2001, Amanda sits there by the Christmas tree like she has done so many years alone and is thinking what her Christmas wish would be this year. I don't know how to explain this but every year on Christmas Eve, she would make a Christmas wish and every year as long as it is not for selfish reasons, Father would grant it. Over the years, most of her wishes were for peace on earth, that the sick would be healed, or that no one would suffer any pain on Christmas Day. So, as she sits there alone, she thinks if she could have any wish at all this year it would be just to see him one last time.

It is December 29, 2001, Amanda has worked until three thirty in the morning. Someone didn't show up for work so she has been there all day and half of the night too. When she wakes up at about 11:00 a.m., she has a fever and is sick. Her husband and the children are bothering her and didn't care that she is sick. Her daughter keeps telling her to go to the store and get some chicken patties. Amanda could not understand why she is being so persistent about it. Amanda finally goes at around 12:45 p.m. Having a fever of a 101 degrees, she really did not feel like doing anything but staying in bed but she goes anyways.

While she is driving there, she keeps seeing Ryan's face in her mind but she didn't understand why. It is almost like she could feel him getting closer to where she is. She pulls up in the parking lot, gets out of the car to go inside when she looks up and sees Ryan walking toward the store. He stops, turns around like he has forgotten something; otherwise, Ryan and Amanda would have been walking in at the same time. When she did see him go back to his car that is when she goes ahead and walks inside. She is not really sure whether he saw her or not.

While she is in the store, she looks down an aisle and sees him standing there looking at the cooler. She so much wants to say something to him but because she looks so terrible and because she has a fever she didn't want to get close to him and make him sick. So she just buys what she needs, leaves the store, and goes to her vehicle. She sits there for a moment and just starts crying, more than anything she wishes she could have heard his voice one last time, but she knew that there must have been a reason for it all. She did, however, say something to Father (God), "Thank you, Father, for granting my wish one last time."

That day, for the first time in Amanda's life, she believed in God again. Through him, she learned that what really matters in this world is that love can change anything and he even said so in his Bible. Greater love has no one than this that he lay down his life for his friends. Amanda will never forget what God gave her, and what he said to her through her mother that came true.

"You will meet a man that you will come to love, and because of that love you will be willing to leave him and give your life for his and in the end, you will believe again."

Now Amanda has never seen Ryan since that day in December, but she knows that as long as she's alive that he will hopefully never die until she does because she gave her life for his. She also knows that someday she will see him again because the Lord said so through Mary, but it will be many years from now. Amanda still has not walked into a church, but someday she will. Hopefully, God will forgive her for not believing in him at first.

If someday the world can let go of the hatred that it carries and believe again, then and only then may God show his mercy on our souls. What we have failed to do is have faith, and because of that, we have lost the real meaning of life.

I know that there will be some that will find it hard to believe that this story is true, but it is and I also know that you must have a lot of questions for Amanda. Such as why was this story not told long ago? What happens to Amanda after this? Does she ever see Ryan again after that day? I also know you have to be wondering where the third message from Mary that she was to give to Amanda is. Most importantly though what is the message that Amanda was told as a child when she died to give to the world? What dreams did she have that she was told to share with the world? Well, don't worry, those are yet to come. These will be in the next book called *Going Past the Darkness and into Amanda's Dreams*. Amanda will then share with the world everything she has been told, what she has seen, and what is to come if we don't change things.

This book is a true story, only the names have been changed to protect those involved. This book is dedicated to (God) Father, in honor of Mary, and to Ryan, whom she loves enough to give her life for. If it isn't for them, Amanda's faith would not have been restored. *Amen*!

ABOUT THE AUTHOR

She was born in the central part of Illinois. She grew up in a time that was much different than it is now. Computers didn't exist, there was no such thing as cell phones, cities were smaller, families sat down and ate together, and the world didn't seem to be moving as fast as it does now. But like everything else, as she grew, things changed over time. She had two children of her own and tried to raise them in a stable family, unlike the one she was born into.

She graduated from high school but went to college not until later in life. As with anyone else, she had times of happiness and sadness. She never gave up hope and thought that her life had a purpose. She always felt that things would get better if only she believed they would. She was happy when her hope and faith guided her to have the one thing she wanted the most—a real family.

CPSIA information can be obtained
at www.ICGtesting.com
Printed in the USA
LVHW090921230521
688258LV00004B/60